Connie,

Thank you so
much for your su...

Enjoy!

Russell Hunt

THE
FORMULA

THE
HOLY BOOK
OF THIS MILLENNIUM

Russell Themagnificent

authorHOUSE®

AuthorHouse™
1663 Liberty Drive
Bloomington, IN 47403
www.authorhouse.com
Phone: 1-800-839-8640

First published by AuthorHouse   01/31/2012

ISBN: 978-1-4685-4857-0 (sc)
ISBN: 978-1-4685-4843-3 (hc)
ISBN: 978-1-4685-4856-3 (ebk)

Library of Congress Control Number: 2012901707

Printed in the United States of America

TABLE OF CONTENTS

This book is dedicated to all freedom-loving freedom fighters, past, present and future.

FOREWORD

THE AGE OF HUMAN ULTIMACY

A *civilization* is the broadest level of common society short of that which distinguishes humans from other species. As such, civilizations may consist of multiple nation-states whose populations possess at their cores common threads distinguishing them from others throughout the world. For example, the United States and Brazil are both independent countries with large diverse populations, separated by thousands of miles. But both countries exist geographically within a larger, more diverse *civilization*, the Western Hemisphere, which spans well over 16 million square miles.

The Western Hemisphere is in fact the Great Demographic Kingdom of Christians upon the Earth—*the Great Kingdom*. The landmass extending from Alaska down to Argentina, including the offshore islands constitutes a demographic kingdom of self-identified Christians. The reality of this kingdom is as much a fact as 2+2=4. Christians of many different denominations are the hemisphere's largest and most widespread constituency, transcending all boundaries, cultural or otherwise. The Great Kingdom, as a civilization, is set apart from others not only by its various regional histories but also by oceans, which physically separate it from the cultural, religious and socio-political groupings of, say, Europe or Asia.

The contiguous independent nation-states of the Western Hemisphere along with the offshore island societies, while unique in their own particular national experiences, constitute mere *fractions* of the hemisphere in which they exist. A wide array of imported and homegrown manifestations of Christianity, disparate but similar indigenous experiences and the admixture of various Old World cultural influences (most notably from, but not limited to, Africa and Europe) are primary determinative elements making the combined populations of the Western Hemisphere a singular *civilization*.

Beginning roughly in the 1500s, modern societies of the Western Hemisphere developed sporadically but concurrently. As such, these societies have commonly inherited a unique intertwining of cultural, political and religious dynamics unseen anywhere else in the world.

The advent of civilizational consciousness, on an elemental level, is emergent in today's world due to humanity's cyclical proclivity to renew itself as times and unforeseen events unfold. Fundamental flaws and deficiencies within well-established structures are now exposed as the agendas associated with secular, religious and political doctrines rapidly play out upon the world stage. Today, as in previous millennia, the crumbling of the perceptual pillars upholding societies has created social, religious and psychological vacuums—vacuums abhorred by human nature.

As trusted institutions deteriorate or disintegrate into mere shells of what they were, humanity's visceral need to partake of something greater and nobler is causing individuals to *yearn* for higher, transcendent levels of identity, personal and otherwise.

As much as anything else, humanity's ability to renew itself is a matter of survival. No doubt; previously established structures were empowering and served useful purposes. But they are proving increasingly inadequate psychically, as the human experience unfolds in unpredictable, subtle, but many times, volatile ways. Simply put, humans need to be *empowered* to view themselves *differently* in this phase of human history.

The new millennium we've entered actually *beckons* for new greatness. Humanity has made extraordinary technological progress over the last several centuries. As a result, culturally, we know far more about each other today than at any other time in history. Literally, mass communication now rests in the palms of individual citizens. No great truth can be hidden or obscured. Today, common citizens with audiences throughout the world have the ability to share great and profound truths with the other inhabitants of the earth—truths that in some cases were obscured for centuries.

What is increasingly obvious is that there is untapped greatness within the mind and spirit of man that must out. There's no telling to what extraordinary heights humanity will rise when the vast greatness hidden within man is revealed—when the unique treasures buried within man are placed on open display for all to see. So far, man has only scratched the surface of his own greatness.

The present-day interpretations of world theologies have grown stale. Times such as these compel the creative genius of humanity to project anew. Newer, better paradigms and standards are transcending older ones. The Great Kingdom, as an operable reality, is foremost in this respect. As the largest Christian civilization in the world, the Great Kingdom is positioned uniquely to champion human civilization at the *highest* possible level.

In 1995, young men from the County of Los Angeles began representing this demographic kingdom as an *institution*, upon a singular foundation: the Law of Christ, which of course is the Law of Love. To this end, this kingdom was committed solely to bringing out the best in humanity by spreading the *sacred formula* contained in this text.

This Millennium is an Age when powerfully transcendent truths and values that only great civilizations can champion will flower. As such, the Great Kingdom is a civilizational torchbearer in this epoch of human history. In recent centuries, the notion of instituting a vast geographical perspective, such as ours, based on something seemingly as subjective and abstract as is the concept of *love* was high fantasy. But yesterday's fantasy is today's reality. Humanity yearns for geographical perspectives—institutional contexts of reality projected upon the earth—whose sole agendas are to inspire, empower and uplift. In this instinctive yearn for higher ground, humanity has shifted gears in dramatic ways throughout the world, transitioning into another phase of its collective experience. Divergent global perspectives now brought to the fore are causing individuals to perceive the world through new lenses. Peoples are asserting their own narratives throughout the world and the idea that any people's narrative should be obscured, shrouded or subjugated, for *whatever* reason, is proving increasingly untenable.

The human instinct is to move ever forward into things that are newer and better. The giant step forward this work represents isn't unique insofar as humanity *always* marches onward, and will continue to do so as long as humans inhabit the earth. What *is* unique is that the kingdom on whose behalf this book was written champions human civilization at its *highest* possible level. This has never been done before.

The Great Kingdom is unmatched in all of human history, and is by far the *greatest* kingdom and civilization of all time! Never in the history of man has there existed an entire kingdom or civilization committed solely to propagating unto the inhabitants of the earth the most powerful elevating phenomenon ever introduced to man.

There has been a centuries-old failure to present to the inhabitants of the earth the eternal principles taught in this work. The human family was deprived of vital information because of this obfuscation. Ignorance, as it relates to the sacred formula you're about to be exposed to, has been very expensive in human costs. It is for this cause that I've undertaken the task of presenting it to you. You'll discover on the following pages an ancient formula hidden in plain view.

More than anything else, THE FORMULA is a manifesto, a literary constitutional representation of that for which this extraordinary millennial kingdom stands: *human ultimacy*. This work was put forth for the sole purpose of bringing individuals face-to-face with the *ultimate* versions of themselves; the *highest* versions of themselves; the *greatest* versions of themselves and the most *wonderful* versions of themselves. In this way, THE FORMULA doesn't only strike the liberation target; it strikes the bull's eye *of* the target. It pierces the mark for the prize, thereby embodying the core spirit of this human epoch. In *this* work, powerful principles obscured for centuries are uncovered for you; and the Great Kingdom, our majestic civilization, is the candlestick upon which the glory now shines.

THE FORMULA is quite simply the most powerful elevating phenomenon ever introduced to man. What you will read on the following pages has the power to revolutionize your life, so let it.

RUSSELL THEMAGNIFICENT

7 August 2007

1

THE
FAMILY
TREASURE

"The Spirit of the Lord God is upon me; because the Lord hath anointed me to preach good tidings unto the meek; he hath sent me to bind up the brokenhearted, to proclaim liberty to the captives, and the opening of the prison to them that are bound; To proclaim the acceptable year of the Lord, and the day of vengeance of our God; to comfort all that mourn . . ."

—Isaiah 61:1-2

PERSONAL IDENTITY

Your personal identity is the most valuable, important and powerful aspect of your life. I'm not referring to your name, nationality or number. Nor am I referring to your biological DNA, ethnicity or family lineage. I'm talking about something far more significant: what you accept and acknowledge as the *truth* about yourself as a unique individual, at this very moment—*inwardly*. I'm talking, with individualized particularity, about your *self*-definition, your *self*-concept, your *self*-perception, your *self*-truth, your *self*-assessment, right now, in this very moment. The personal identity aspect of your own mind is a treasure-chest, the contents of which will either bless or curse you. That which is contained in this specific dimension of your own mind has the ability to bring the best or the worst out of you; it can exalt or debase you. Your personal identity is the determinative program of your life; make no mistake about this.

Your personal life produces an outcome and a quality according to *what* you are, not who you are. *Who* you are will never change. You'll always be the son or daughter of your parents, the brother or sister of your siblings, and so on. Your *biology* is immutable. But your self-*assessment*, what you accept and acknowledge as the truth about yourself *inwardly*, as a unique individual, at this very moment, can change—*instantly*. The distinction between what you are and who you are is an important one. The principle underscored by this distinction is the first of two premier laws governing the human experience—the *Law of Destiny*.

THE LAW OF DESTINY

The Law of Destiny is **Identity Produces Destiny**. Simply put, what a thing *is* determines what it can and will produce. The apple tree was an apple tree long before it brought forth apples. The sprouting of a tree's fruit doesn't *determine* what manner of tree it is; it simply *reveals* what manner of tree it is. The original *seed* determined the manner of tree.

The tree was *already* an apple tree. It was never *becoming* an apple tree. It was all it was ever going to be when only a foot high, with no branches, leaves or apples. Even when there was no visible evidence of what it was, when its identity was a complete mystery, the tree wasn't any less what it was than when it came into full bloom. It was what it was—*already*, and because of what it was, its life simply produced accordingly. What others thought of it was irrelevant. What others said about it was irrelevant. What was growing contemporaneously in its environs made no difference. It was already everything it was ever going to be, irrespective of all else. Though it had to endure multiple fruitless seasons, it was only a matter of time until the tree's life bore witness to what it had long been. Put simply, the reason a tree produces apples is because it's an apple tree—*already*. So it is with you.

What your life produces doesn't *determine* what manner of individual you are; it *reveals* it. The manner of individual you are *inwardly* determines what your life can and will produce *outwardly*. Your actions, choices and decisions are not the *sources* of your destiny. Philosophical positions that assert as much are utterly false. Actions, choices and decisions are the *products* of your identity. It may appear as though the branch is the source of the apple because the stem attached to the apple grows visibly from the branch; but in reality, the branch itself is as much a *product* of the original seed as is the apple.

Identity is the source of destiny! How you define yourself constitutes the basis underlying why you do what you do, choose what you choose and decide what you decide. Actions, choices and decisions are just as much *products* of your identity as is the destiny they aid in manifesting. They are outgrowths of identity, mere functions of identity. Doing is a function of being, not the other way around. In all your conscious living experiences, you acted in accordance to the dictates of your personal identity. In other words, you did what you did *because* of your self-definition. This is why ultimately, in order to control your destiny, you must control your *identity*. Your life is not a product of what you do; it's a product of what you *are*.

Your personal identity is nothing but a seed. If you were to cut an apple seed in half, you obviously will not find an apple tree. But an entire orchard is contained within a single seed. Though the seed is small enough to fit on the tip of your finger, it actually has the potential to produce unlimited apples trees. The apple seed contains DNA, the genetic blueprint necessary for specific reproduction. Remaining true to the reproductive power of one single apple seed can produce thousands of acres of apple trees. The same principle applies to your personal identity. Your self-concept contains a destiny structure, DNA, a specific blueprint. This structure empowers your identity to produce the *fruit* of its origin. I'll come back to this point shortly.

Destiny structure consists of seven primary elements: state of mind, perspective, agenda, attitude, aura, words and action. Taken in order, your state of mind is your thought, your level of consciousness, the inclination and trajectory of your mental activity as it relates to all around you. Your perspective is not so much what you see, but *how* you see it. Your agenda is your purpose, your program of intent. Your attitude is the psychological disposition with which you approach your life. Your aura is your gravitational force, the personal polarity causing you to attract and repel. Your words reveal not only what you say and how you say it, but also what you don't say and how you don't say it. Your actions reveal not only what you do and how you do it, but also what you don't do and how you don't do it. There are other elements and dimensions of destiny structure, but they are *sub-categories* of these primary elements. Your destiny structure, taken together, is the specific genetic material that produces the outcome and quality of your living experience; it's the DNA of your identity, which produces your destiny.

Philosophers, religionists and intellectuals alike have deified one or more elements of destiny structure, assigning to these elements greater status than they are due. These individuals have struck the *target* of the mysteries surrounding personal destiny but have missed the *mark*. In print are many volumes written on various elements of destiny structure. I'm obviously not suggesting these elements aren't worthy of the written word; however, to present them as *sources* of destiny rather than mere *products* of identity is misleading and potentially harmful. As important as these vital elements are, both individually and in concert with each other, in no way do they constitute the *sources* of destiny. Again, they are mere *products* of identity. The only way to control these elements is to control your personal identity, which is their source.

Your personal identity is by far the most significant aspect of your life. No personal identity is benign, no personal identity powerless. All identities contain a destiny structure, a specific genetic blueprint that individual lives inevitably obey in proportion to the extent to which they are embraced. This is an immutable principle that was set in motion upon the earth at the beginning of time. As your identity goes, so goes your destiny. That which controls your identity also controls your destiny. This is why *you* must be in control of your personal identity, which brings us to the second of the two premier laws governing the human experience.

THE LAW OF HUMAN NATURE

The second of the premier laws governing the human experience is the Law of Human Nature: *Identity Selectivity*. This is the companion principle to the Law of Destiny. Identity produces destiny, *but* man has identity options. Man has the ability and the right to *select* his own personal identity based on three dimensions of time: the past, the present, or a vision—a conception—of the future. But regardless of the dimension of time from which a man selects his personal identity, those elements will reproduce corresponding fruit in *his* future, beginning now. This is why a man must be careful, because if you define yourself based on elements of the past, your life is going to *reproduce* corresponding fruit in your future, beginning now. You'll repeatedly find yourself in the same situations operating with the same destiny structure, and producing the same results. Your life will be a repetitive cycle, and depending on what that cycle consists of, this may or may not prove a positive thing for you. "Be not deceived; God is not mocked: for whatsoever a man soweth, that shall he also reap."[1] The key word in this passage is *"that,"* because if you plant *that*, you're not going to harvest *this*, and vice-versa. This universal truth applies to all life. Identity is the seed of destiny; but unlike other life forms, humans have the distinct privilege of *choosing* what that seed will be.

Your destiny is not a matter of chance; it's not a gamble; it's a *science*, but you must understand it in order to control it. Fixed laws and principles govern all life. However, these laws and principles can be harnessed in the service of man. Man has the ability and the right to *select* his own personal identity, which gives him personal authority over the outcome and quality of his own living experience—his personal *destiny* on earth, beginning right here, right now, in this very moment.

What you presently accept and acknowledge as the truth about yourself *inwardly* determines what your life can and will produce *outwardly*. The extent to which you are true to any identity is the extent to which that identity will be true to you. The elements of which your personal identity consists will reproduce in your future according to their origin, in exact

---

[1] GALATIANS 6:7 (All biblical references are from the Authorized King James Version)

proportion to your embrace. As a human being, you do have free will, exercised in your choice of identities and the range of options revealed by the destiny structure contained *within* any given identity.

The relevant question is not so much, "*What* did your personal identity come from?" but "*When* did your personal identity come from—past, present or a vision of your future?" From what manner of fruit was your personal identity extracted—*chronologically*? This question is important because the origin of your personal identity is indicative of the destiny your life is producing right now.

Your life has no choice but to reproduce the elements and dimensions of your personal identity's fruit of origin. A seed can only produce the fruit it comes from. It's futile to *act* in the hopes for something new in life while holding on to an identity that doesn't correspond to that for which you are hoping. All such empty action, forcefully taken in an identity for which it doesn't correspond, is vacuous. You'll just be going through the motions. Your actions will have no power.

It's been said generally that a man must control his thoughts about this or that thing in order to control his destiny; but I say unto you that a man must control his thoughts about *himself* in order to control his destiny. "For as he thinketh in his heart, so is he."[2] The term *"heart"* symbolizes the *identity* dimension of a man's mind. Your thoughts concerning the issues and things of life will always be in accordance with what you *are*—inwardly. They will be in accordance with what you accept and acknowledge as the truth about *yourself*. Your

---

[2]   PROVERBS 23:7

personal identity will always be the basis of what you think of all else.

It's been said that insanity is repeatedly doing the same thing but expecting different results. But I say to you that insanity is repeatedly *being* the same thing but expecting different results. You've heard it said that individuals must take responsibility for their actions, choices and decisions. But I say to you that individuals must take responsibility for their *identities*. You may have heard the slogan, "Just do it." But I declare to you, "Just be it." To *do* anything you must first *be* something. Those who *do* something in particular are those who *are* something in particular. You can only do according to what you are. The potential within you to act, choose or decide *effectively* is determined by what you are *definitively*. If it's not *in* you, it can't proceed *from* you. This should be clear enough.

Volitionally, there are things in this life you will do and things you simply will not do. It's not that you lack the opportunity or physical ability to do those things. The activities you won't engage in are simply inconsistent with your personal identity. Those activities don't correspond with what you accept and acknowledge about yourself, inwardly. They are outside the range of structural options made available to you by your self-concept. There are things no amount of money can get you to do; they're off the table and non-negotiable. Those activities are beyond the limits established by your self-concept. In fact, they're not even up for discussion. There are others, however, who won't hesitate to engage in those activities. What is abjectly unacceptable behavior while operating in one identity is perfectly acceptable in another. In this way, any personal identity is both constraining and liberating, both inhibiting and empowering.

There is a distinct gravitational force surrounding your personal identity. There is an aura surrounding your personal being. Others can detect the energy. The force of your being has such strength that others can hear what you said with their eyes and see what you did with their ears. It's been said that actions speak louder than words. This may be true on some levels, but *being* speaks louder and conveys more forcefully than words or actions. The unspoken and the unseen are detected sublimely. Others can *sense* what manner of man you are; they can sense your character. The *spirit* of your presence speaks louder and more clearly than any words from your mouth or any overt conscious action on your part.

There is a polarity that accompanies your personal identity—an invisible push and pull. Certain people and things are attracted to you, while others are repelled. The maintenance of your friends and enemies relies on your personal identity. The more your friends discover about you, the more they'll love and appreciate you. The more your enemies discover about you, the more they'll detest and despise you. You may have met unrepentant individuals of whom your instincts gave immediate warning. You may not have witnessed any nefarious act they committed, but you could *sense* the act on them. Wherever they go, they unknowingly carry the spirit of the identity that produced that act. The act itself may have been committed long ago in some distant locale, but the aura of the identity that *produced* the act lives on. The same dynamic reveals those who have privately engaged in wonderful deeds. In strange and peculiar ways, that which is done in darkness comes to light, revealing both that which is evil and that which is good.

Many things can shape and mold personal identity. A primary influence is an individual's family background. A family's unique history or experience may dramatically affect those born into it. Individuals are born into all sorts of family scenarios. A family's collective character was shaped and molded long before the current generations even came onto the scene. The effects of a family's experiences are passed down through inter-generational relationships and sometimes through the *lack* of inter-generational relationships. Strangely, many times it's not those who are present who most affect the character of a family, but those who are absent.

It's possible for a wonderful family legacy to be handed from one generation to the next. The extent or absence of one generation's relationship with another is pivotal in determining the extent to which previous experiences impact ensuing generations. Whether positive or negative, a family's previous experiences have an effect on those born into it. The effects of previous events are transferred and somehow woven into an individual's psyche. While the effects may be incomprehensible consciously, they are present nonetheless.

Cultural background can shape an individual's personal identity. There are cultures that possess long, glorious histories. These cultures have great legacies of victory and triumph. Individuals born into these cultures can't help but be exposed to their inherited glory. The history is proudly handed from one generation to the next. This sort of cultural background can provide a sense of pride, honor and self-esteem within an individual.

But there are also cultures that have experienced nothing but pain, tragedy and degradation. Individuals born into these cultures are inevitably exposed to their degraded place on the social scale and to low expectations. This can be a source of great shame and of distorted, mutated self-concepts.

Different aspects of an individual's personal living experience can shape his personal identity. Situations, circumstances, environments, events, social realities and human interaction of all sorts can contribute to what an individual inwardly accepts and acknowledges as *self*-truth.

Substance abuse is an experience that can shape personal identity. The self-concept of an addict may be so severely altered that viewing him in the midst of active addiction versus at other times is like the difference between night and day. Many times, even when an addict is clean, evidence of previous abuse is revealed in his character and behavior. This is because foreign substances have indelibly distorted his self-concept. His destiny structure has been altered. The wonderful people and elements that once orbited him no longer do. Due to a changed destiny structure, his life produces something different than it would have otherwise.

Traumatic events of all kinds can shape personal identity. This is particularly true for children. The childhood loss of one or both parents can permanently shape a person's self-concept. Some carry scars from childhood trauma for the remainder of their lives.

War is known to shape, mold and even damage personal identity. Both combatants and civilian victims of war have been known to have their personal identities damaged or altered in tragic ways by the ravages of combat.

In short, life presents an individual with a constant tug-of-war over the critical element of *personal identity*. Most have some degree of vulnerability in this regard. Ultimately, if your *self*-concept is not more powerful than the images and conceptions others project upon and around you, you will unconsciously internalize external madness. You'll absorb the thoughts and impressions others have of you into your own consciousness and begin to reflect them in your life. It's possible to be so overcome with the thoughts of others concerning you that you'll actually define yourself through *their* eyes, and with greater intensity than *they* do. This is how unspoken projections and the associated expectations of situations, circumstances and environments can powerfully affect the lives of individuals.

In one social-pressure experiment I participated in, the facilitator placed a strip of tape on the foreheads of individuals in a group seated in a circle. On each strip of tape was inscribed a brief *self-definition*, though no one was privy to the inscription attached to their own forehead. The self-definitions were not to be told or alluded to in any way; but participants were instructed specifically to *treat* each person according to the attachment on his or her forehead. The facilitator then initiated open discussion among the group and instructed group members to interact freely among themselves. Interestingly, as the interaction progressed, individual group participants began to *internalize* how other members of the group were treating them. Over several minutes, group members actually began to reflect, or respond in some way to, the characteristics affixed to their own foreheads.

In this same exercise was a very homely, plain-looking young lady. But the inscription on the strip of tape attached to her forehead said, "I'm very beautiful; everyone loves me." She was unaccustomed to this treatment and had an immediate demonstrable reaction to the attention she received. She was clearly suspicious and uncomfortable as group members began fawning over her whenever the conversation turned her way. What was noteworthy was that about 15 minutes into the session, it became clear that she was actually beginning to *feel* beautiful. Her suspicion gradually dissipated. She was becoming increasingly comfortable in her interaction with the others. At one point, she actually reached into her purse for a brush and began brushing her hair. She began to sit upright as though on display, beaming with beauty, reflecting what group members were projecting. She became more lively and bubbly. In less than a half hour, this young lady fully *internalized* the beauty projected onto her by the others and began to conduct herself accordingly. I can't tell this story without hastening to add that she appeared none too pleased when the exercise ended. Humans are vulnerable in this way, both positively and negatively.

Many times good intentions go awry; wonderful talents go to waste and honorable upbringing is cast aside because individuals are exposed to overwhelming pressure to conform or to fit in to something. The pressure, as was revealed in the group exercise, doesn't have to be verbalized in order to be applied; it may only be *implied*. Individuals can detect the expectations of their environments and in their interpersonal relationships. Many struggle to stand against the expectations projected by others.

Children have a particularly high level of identity-vulnerability. One doesn't have to verbalize high or low expectations in order for a child to internalize them. A child has an instinctive level of sentience, especially active in the relationships with his or her parents and teachers. A child will internalize unspoken expectations against his or her conscious will. In this way, a child may be elevated or condemned silently through subtle but powerful expectations.

Individuals who are particularly at risk, for whatever reason, need to understand the value, importance and power of personal identity. The lack of knowledge as it relates to the *nexus* between personal identity and personal destiny is set-up for disaster. The price one pays for ignorance in this regard is very high. When individuals don't understand the cause and effect relationship between identity and destiny, it can lead to what has been termed *learned helplessness*. Individuals will surrender themselves completely to the elements and forces surrounding them, without even realizing it. Destruction is the inevitable result.

According to the National Center for Health Statistics, suicide in the United States is the eleventh ranked cause of death, with a rate higher than homicide.[3] This statistic refers to *common* suicide: the deliberate taking of one's own life. All that

---

[3]   Jarrett Bell, Tragedy forces Dungy 'to live in the present,' <u>USA Today</u>, 1-4 September 2006: 2A

some may deem suicide, however, may not be direct, immediate or even deliberate. Most self-destructive behavior is drawn out over a period of years and can be deceptively gradual, destroying life in subtle, sometimes imperceptible, ways. Destructive, self-minimizing thoughts and behavior, more often than not, are the result of outside influences *combined* with ignorance of the power or possibilities of personal identity.

Super Bowl champion head coach Tony Dungy gave an interview eight months following the suicide death of his eldest son, James, who was 18-years-old. One can only imagine the pain and anguish of this grieving father as he soul-searched for answers. During the interview, he shared his deeply felt thoughts on what had become a growing problem. "I think young people are struggling with their identity. What really makes them tick? What's important to them? We're getting a lot of conflicted messages. That's one thing that we, as a society, have to get across to our young guys: How are you going to be defined? Are you defined by being successful at work? By being an All-American or a Pro Bowler? Is that what makes us, or is it something different? Hopefully, we can get across to them that it's something different. It's what you are internally."[4] Coach Dungy could not have been more on point.

The second of the two premier laws governing the human experience holds that you have the ability and the right to *choose* your personal identity. Your ability to change your personal identity is based on the Law of Human Nature, the prime principle that distinguishes humans from other species. You have the ability and the right to seize full control of the

---

[4]   Ibid

identity aspect of your own mind. This is what enables you to gain full control of your personal destiny. You have the right to a specifically designed, tailor-made personal identity—one that will *produce* the unique vision you have for your own life.

The treasure of the apple isn't its size, taste or color. The treasure of the apple is the seed within it. The apple is for consumption, but the seed within it is for production. A seed's power is limited in one critical respect. It can only reproduce the manner of fruit from which it proceeded. Metaphorically speaking, the treasure of the grand vision you have for your life is not its size, taste or color. The treasure of the hope of your life is the seed contained within it: the identity of victory *within* your vision of victory. Remember, this identity, like any other, is nothing but a seed. But in this case, it's the *only* seed that can actually produce your dream. This seed is your personal blessing, the *ultimate* version of you. It's your treasure because it's the only thing that actually has the power to *produce* the highest possible living experience available to you—the highest possible level of freedom and liberation available to you, beginning right here in this very moment. Remember, destiny, like any other manifestation of life, is a product of a particular *type* of seed.

Life isn't merely about accessing a simple successful version of you. Conventional off-the-rack identities can produce simple success in any given activity. *Ultimacy*, which is what you have a right to experience, is about obtaining and then operating in the *ultimate* version of you; the *highest* version of you; the *greatest* version of you; the most *wonderful* version of you; the *Almighty's* version of you, right here, right now, in this very moment. Anything less is unacceptable and a *waste* of your precious time!

THE BLESSING OF ABRAHAM

Now that you understand the two premier principles governing the human experience, it's time for you to activate the sacred formula of the blessing of Abraham in your life. This sacred formula is the most powerful elevating and transformational phenomenon ever introduced to man. It is, and has always been, a dramatic life-changing revolutionary formula. It has the power to transform a man from the rock bottoms of his life to the tip-top of his life—from dust and dunghill to throne of glory, right here, right now, in this very moment.

Begin by answering the Blessing Question. This profound question—in light of the premier principles governing the human experience—actually reveals and brings you face-to-face with your *personal blessing*, the *ultimate* version of you. Your answers to the Blessing Question actually reveal the great blessing of Abraham as it applies to your individual life. Understand that the blessing of Abraham is a *kind* of blessing, a *sort* of blessing, a *type* of blessing that is thousands of years old. It's an individualized blessing designed to highly accentuate the contours of your personal living experience, to accentuate divinely the specific dynamics of your individual personal existence. It's a tailor-made blessing, designed to fit you only. By answering the Blessing Question, you're submitting yourself to a personal fitting from the Almighty Tailor. The blessing of Abraham is not a one-size-fits-all phenomenon. It's not an off-the-rack sort of blessing; no one gets the exact same thing. This isn't a cookie-cutter, general-application blessing; everyone is prescribed something uniquely different. The Blessing Question brings you into a divine moment of personal discovery. This very moment is your moment of truth, and you should experience it in the fullness of your glory. The following is the most significant question you'll ever answer in life:

> ## "What is your most glorious self-definition in your vision of your victorious future?"

What exactly did you achieve—not in your past but—in your vision of your victorious future? Now, define yourself in the most glorious and wonderful terms, *based* on what you actually achieved in your vision. At the stage of manifested victory, what *would* be your most glorious self-definition, your most glorious self-assessment, your most glorious self-truth? If your dream came true in full, and not only were you blessed, but everyone else was as well, what would you say about you, *to you*—then? Get a sheet of paper and write down every answer that comes to mind. Don't hold back! Pour out your soul. When you're done, come back to this place. Stop reading now; think about the question and begin writing.

Welcome back. Now that you've finished answering the Blessing Question, take a good look at what you've written. What you've written down on that sheet of paper is your *personal blessing*. It is the revelation of the blessing of Abraham in and for your life. What you've written down is the *ultimate* version of you. It's you indeed, but it's the *highest* version of you. This is the identity of victory *extracted* from your own vision of victory. It constitutes the seed you've identified within your own victorious vision. This is the *identity dimension* of your faith, the main ingredient of your faith. This is your seed. This is "the substance of things hoped for, the evidence of things not seen"[5] for you in this life. This seed can only reproduce the manner of fruit from which it came; it has no other choice. If you plant this seed in the soil of your mind right now, it will immediately turn your life into this kind of tree. This tree will have no choice but to reproduce the fruit from which it came. In this case, the fruit from which you extracted your seed was your vision of victory. If you embrace that identity of victory as your personal identity right now, your life will not only *be* that kind of tree, but will *produce* your vision of victory.

This is "the promise of the Spirit through faith"[6]: The identity of victory extracted from your vision of victory but embraced in the present with absolute confidence will *produce* your vision of victory. The extent to which you remain true to your identity of victory is the extent to which it will remain true to you. You must fully embrace your personal blessing as your personal identity right now, with absolute confidence.

---

[5]   HEBREWS 11:1
[6]   GALATIANS 3:14

Shine with the glory of your personal blessing at all times by operating in it fully. Be what your personal blessing reveals right now. Understanding the two premier principles that govern the human experience will enable you to operate confidently in your personal blessing without wavering.

It's not about becoming in order to be; it's about *being* in order to become. The Almighty never calls anything to become; He calls things to be. He never said, "Let there become light." He said, "Let there be light."[7] He "calleth those things which be not as though they were,"[8] not as though they should *become*. There's no transformative power in becoming; the power is always in being. When it comes to your self-concept, you actually *are*, and are not *becoming*. When it comes to your personal identity, you're not becoming anything. You're not going to be anything. It's not a matter of what you could be, should be or would be. It's always a matter of what you *are* right now—inwardly, because what you are right now determines the outcome and quality of your entire living experience.

Fully embrace your personal blessing as your personal identity right now, with absolute confidence. Honor the Law of Destiny and the Law of Human Nature. Redefine yourself on a glorious level, as it is your God-given right to do. Your desired destiny won't be manufactured through artifice or manifest by happenstance; it will be an authentic outgrowth of your living experience.

The reason the Almighty introduced this phenomenon to man in the first place is twofold. First, He knew man would

---

[7]   GENESIS 1:3
[8]   ROMANS 4:17

degrade himself. He knew man would increasingly cheapen himself and come to operate in a low-grade version of himself if he weren't exposed to a higher reality. Second, man is at his best when he's glorious and victorious. It's the Almighty's will that man be at his best, which is why it was important that this sacred formula be introduced into the human experience. Humanity needed it. There is no need to be intimidated or frightened by the novelty of this phenomenon. While it may be new to you, it has been with man for millennia and is fully tried and tested.

For a deeper understanding of the phenomenon, let's take a few minutes to look back at its origins.

ABRAM'S EXPERIENCE

Long ago, there lived a man whose name was Abram. He had an extraordinary, seemingly ridiculous, vision for his life. The vision called for his offspring to be as numerous as the stars of the sky and as multitudinous as the grains of sand on the seashore. Through his offspring and through his personal experience, Abram was to *be* a blessing to all the families of the earth. Abram's problem was that he and his wife, Sarai, had no children; and Sarai had been unable to bear children all her life. To top it off, they both were now well beyond childbearing years. He was 99; she was 90. At the behest of Sarai, Abram had already fathered a son through her bondservant, a fertile woman whose name was Hagar. Their son's name was Ishmael. But Abram's original vision was for Sarai to bear his seed.

Abram had no answer to *this* dilemma. He was holding on to a seemingly impossible dream. How was his wife Sarai going to bear seed out of season? Her window of opportunity had long passed. Certainly, he thought, Ishmael is the embodiment of his vision and of the divine legacy.

Though he didn't realize it, Abram was about to come into the highest realm of eternal truth—higher than any truth he had ever known. He was about to learn the Law of Destiny and the Law of Human Nature. Divine wisdom was about to be introduced into the human family through the lives of Abram and Sarai. At 99 years old, Abram received the ultimate wisdom. The Almighty spoke to him and said, "As for me, behold, my covenant is with thee, and thou shalt be a father of many nations. Neither shall thy name any more be called Abram, but thy name shall be Abraham; for a father of many nations have I made thee."[9] Notice, "*have* I made thee" is past tense. The Almighty called Abram something that he was *not* as though he *were*. The name Abraham actually means "father of many nations," but there was no visible evidence of this in Abram's life.

The Most High went on to declare, "As for Sarai thy wife, thou shalt not call her name Sarai, but Sarah shall her name be. And I will bless her . . . and she shall be a mother of nations; kings of people shall be of her."[10] The name Sarah actually means "princess." Abram complied fully. Through this revelation, the Almighty introduced Abram to the two premier laws governing

---

[9] GENESIS 17:4-5
[10] GENESIS 17:15-16

the human experience. This wisdom constitutes the basis of the sacred formula of *the blessing of Abraham.*

To this day, the blessing of Abraham—a particular *type* of blessing—remains the most powerful elevating and transformational phenomenon ever introduced into the human experience. The blessing of Abraham is *human ultimacy*, reflecting mastery of the Law of Destiny and the Law of Human Nature. It's through this phenomenon that humanity received knowledge of the full concept of what's known as *now faith.* Embracing the personal identity of *Abraham* was Abram's *now faith:* the substance of things hoped for, the evidence of things not seen—for *Abram.* Abraham was the *ultimate* version of Abram, thus, Abraham could produce what Abram could not. Abraham was the first to experience and articulate this phenomenon. This is why Abraham is the historical father of the faith phenomenon.

Of all the wisdom introduced to man throughout the ages, *nothing* rises to the revelatory pinnacle represented by the blessing of Abraham. Universally, Abraham is referred to as *the patriarch of faith*, and he is. But even from a purely secular or academic perspective, Abraham could justifiably be called *the patriarch of philosophy.* The word "philosophy" literally means *love of wisdom.* Unlike Abraham, none of the highly reputed philosophers (lovers of wisdom) of history was able to champion the two premier laws. These laws constitute the height of divine wisdom. Abraham lived in circa 2000 BC. There is no evidence that common philosophers, educators or religionists—before or since—even knew of these eternal laws, much less revealed them to the rest of humanity.

For Abram, the blessing of *Abraham* was a profound revelation. He came to understand that his extraordinary, seemingly impossible, vision wasn't dependent upon his vast wealth or on what he was or wasn't doing. He understood for the first time that his desired destiny was solely dependent upon his *personal identity*. It was solely dependent upon what he presently accepted and acknowledged as the truth about *himself*—inwardly, as a unique individual in this life—right here, right now, in this very moment.

As was customary of the times, Abram's given name had a meaning. It was indicative of a "self-definition" assigned to him at birth. Abram actually means *high father*. What this tells us is that Abram already had a wonderful personal identity, an identity that garnered him high repute and great wealth. Abram already had a robust and effective personal identity. But *high father* wasn't nearly as great as *father of many nations*. One identity was ordinary, the other extraordinary. Abram discovered that all he ever needed in order for his extraordinary vision to manifest was an extraordinary personal identity—a greater, more glorious self-concept extracted directly from the vision itself. Abram needed to be exposed to the *ultimate* version of himself. The new identity that Abram embraced wasn't extracted from past or present elements or realities. His new personal identity—Abraham—was based on and extracted from his own vision of his victorious future. *Abraham* was the identity of victory extracted from Abram's vision of victory but embraced by Abram in the present, with absolute confidence.

Abraham was Abram's most glorious self-definition in his vision of his victorious future. The key was for Abram to throw off the identity of Abram and to embrace fully the identity of *Abraham* in the present, with absolute confidence. And this is what he did. Abram instantly became the *father of many nations* by accepting and acknowledging *Abraham* as the truth about himself in the present tense. Abraham's transformation wasn't a gradual process. He became by being. His new identity was the substance of what he was hoping for, the evidence of what he could not see with his natural sight. The Law of Destiny caused his life to produce according to what he *now* was. He was able to produce now what he couldn't produce before, because *he* was now something that he wasn't before.

Sarai also required a new identity. How was a 90-year-old barren woman going to conceive and give birth to a child? What strange phenomenon could trump even the common course of human reproductive nature? Abraham redefined his wife—a redefinition she accepted. At 90-years-old, Sarai instantly became *Sarah*. Sarah's new personal identity indicated that she was now a fertile *princess*, a queen mother of kings and nations. They were consecrated as husband and wife for a singular purpose. They were *one* in the enterprise of life and in the miracle they were about to experience. Sarah was Sarai's identity of victory, her most glorious self-definition extracted from the vision of victory she shared with her husband. Abraham began calling her something that she was not as though she were. She then began calling *herself* something that she was not as though she were.

According to the story, Sarah found the notion of producing a child at her advanced age a bit amusing. Nonetheless, she fully embraced *Sarah* as her personal identity—in the present.

Again, this was not a gradual process. Sarah became by *being*, and as you'll see, the Law of Destiny caused her life to produce accordingly.

Abram and Sarai were the first individuals in recorded human history endowed with this particular phenomenon. It is important to note that it was the Law of Human Nature that enabled Abram and Sarai to *choose* Abraham and Sarah as their personal identities. It was, in the final analysis, *their* choices, as personal identity is always an individual choice. They exercised their ability and right to redefine themselves in the present based on their own vision of their victorious future. In a matter of months, their activation of the blessing formula would cause Abraham and Sarah to produce what Abram and Sarai could never produce: a miracle-child. *Isaac* was the son born to them, the son of the "promise of the Spirit through faith."

It's also important to note that while Isaac was the very embodiment of Abram's glorious vision, *Abram* could not produce him. Only *Abraham* could produce Isaac. Only *Abraham* could produce Abram's vision. The identity that conceives a great vision is *not* the identity that produces it. Identity change is a necessary aspect of the blessing phenomenon.

The vision the Almighty gave to *Abram* thousands of years ago continues to manifest to this day, through Christ, who was himself a product of *Abraham* according to lineage. The sacred formula by which Isaac was conceived was passed from generation to generation through the millennia, down to you, its present-day trustee. Now receive the blessing formula, the most powerful elevating phenomenon ever introduced to man:

> The identity of victory extracted from your vision of victory but embraced in the present with absolute confidence.

This is it and this is all. Read it repeatedly. The ultimate purpose of handing this phenomenon down through the generations was for it to be a *gift* to all the families of the earth. This sacred formula is an everlasting blessing unto all humanity. It unleashes untapped greatness buried within. It catapults individuals into the greatest dimensions of personal reality. It empowers individuals to manifest the most unlikely dreams and aspirations. It sets in motion self-revolutions that transcend the most dire situations, circumstances and environments. It brings individuals face-to-face with the *ultimate* versions of themselves. Human ultimacy, which is what the blessing of Abraham manifests, is what life on earth is all about in this Great Millennium and beyond. This is why the blessing formula is so important to all humanity.

This is the same sacred formula that produced all the Hebrew kings and prophets of the Bible. They were all descendants of Abraham—actual *products* of the promise of the Spirit through faith. This phenomenal inheritance brought them face-to-face with the ultimate versions of themselves and enabled them to flourish in spite of dire contradictory situations, circumstances, environments and events. It was also to this phenomenon they could return whenever they fell into degradation and unrighteousness. This phenomenon is the royal family's great inheritance, which means that it's *your* inheritance.

Paul, the great Christian apostle to the Gentiles, once wrote, "Christ hath redeemed us from the curse of the law . . . That the blessing of Abraham might come on the Gentiles through Jesus Christ; that we might receive the promise of the Spirit through faith."[11] That is to say, Jesus, who was himself a direct descendant of Abraham, intended his extraordinary personal sacrifice to be the catalyst by which this particular phenomenon would spread unto all the inhabitants of the earth.

There is obviously more to the Christian doctrine than life after death. It also includes an extraordinary provision for life *before* death. The blessing of Abraham has nothing at all to do with life after death, but *everything* to do with life on earth. It has everything to do with bringing you face-to-face with the ultimate version of you—right here, right now, in this very moment.

Abram was the chosen vessel through whom man was introduced to this phenomenon. Man required the keys to an elevated personal consciousness in order to flourish despite overwhelming contradictory stimuli. Abram, before he became Abraham, could be trusted as a custodian of this formula. He could be trusted not only to receive but to also exemplify and impart this sacred wisdom, which is precisely what he did. Abram's faithfulness is why this phenomenon is the blessing of *Abraham*. This powerful blessing is our family's legacy—our

---

[11]   GALATIANS 3:13-14; See also GENESIS 28:4 for first mention.

family's great treasure; and our patriarch Abraham is the *father* of the phenomenon.

ESAU, THE FOOLISH GRANDSON

From the beginning, not everyone in Abraham's family had an appreciation for the family's treasure. Abraham's grandson, Esau, despised his birthright. It was the right of Isaac's firstborn to be entrusted with the family's sacred formula. Esau was supposed to inherit custody and experience ultimacy in order to pass his knowledge and personal testimony on. It was to be his job to make sure the sacred formula was handed down faithfully to ensuing generations.

But Esau didn't have an appreciation for his own inheritance. He didn't appreciate the importance of what his family's duty was upon the earth. Esau sold his birthright to Jacob, his younger twin, for a bite to eat. The fact that he considered the family's sacred formula a mere commodity that could or should be sold off, even to his own brother, disqualified him from being custodian of the legacy. For this, he is called *profane*.[12] The blessing of Abraham is a sacred inheritance given to Abraham's line by the Almighty Himself. It is a prized possession, but Esau despised it. Certainly, he knew that some powerful phenomenon produced a miracle through his grandparents. Even if he didn't know exactly what the formula was, he owed his very existence to the phenomenon. His father's birth was nothing short of a

---

[12]   HEBREWS 12:16

supernatural event, a miracle. This alone should've spawned a desire to inherit custody of the family's legacy, but it didn't.

Families who inherit great legacies must be careful of their generational custodians. One individual's disvalue of the family's legacy can result in loss of the legacy. One walks away from what one does not value. The descendants of Esau, who did in fact become a large nation, never experienced the phenomenon of *ultimacy*. The Edomites remained a bitter, mediocre lot whom history has largely forgotten. They would've been extraordinary, but for their birth into a foolish patriarch's inability to appreciate what was truly important.

Although Jacob wasn't in line to inherit custody of the sacred formula, he had an appreciation for what was happening through his family. So he purchased rights to the formula in order to exemplify and perpetuate it. Jacob knew what was important. His methods were dubious, but his priorities were in order. To be sure, he used cunning manipulation to obtain the sacred formula, but he knew intuitively that his twin would sell it.

Rebekeh, the twins' mother, also considered the family's legacy more important than did he whose right it was to possess it. Through deceptive means, she actually facilitated the process of Jacob acquiring the legacy. Though it was Isaac's wish that Esau inherit the sacred formula, it was not to be. And Rebekeh worked to ensure this.

THE SECRET RECIPE

All secret recipes consist of common ingredients mixed in uncommon ways. There are highly successful food and beverage companies that manufacture products using secret recipes known only to a few trusted individuals. These recipes are trade secrets. It's important to recognize that the ingredients used to make these products aren't imported from other planets. They're quite common right here on earth. What makes these products unique is the special way the ingredients are mixed. The *recipe* is the treasure, not the ingredients.

The blessing of Abraham consists of common ingredients put together in an uncommon way. Personal identity is a common element. What one accepts and acknowledges about oneself inwardly as a unique individual, in this very moment, is something with which everyone is familiar. Desired destiny, the hoped-for outcome and quality of one's own living experience, is a common concept. It's common for individuals to nurture a personal hope for the future. Among human beings, dreams, goals, aspirations and hopes are commonplace. There are many volumes written on these subjects.

What makes the sacred formula unique is that it's the identity of victory extracted from your vision of victory but embraced in the present—that is, *right now in this very moment*—with absolute confidence! It is the self-concept taken from your own victorious vision of the future, but confidently and wholeheartedly embracing it in the present. For some, this may seem like a meaningless, foolish or presumptuous proposition. The fact that it's even possible to redefine yourself in the present based on your own vision of your victorious future may stretch your mind a bit. Most don't realize that it's possible, or even *feasible*, to do such a thing. This phenomenon calls for you to operate fully in an identity that contradicts everything in your past or present visible realities. The activation of the sacred formula may seem impractical, illogical or even insane, but this phenomenon is actually the most powerful elevating phenomenon ever introduced to man. Never forget that identity produces destiny.

Valuing this formula is vital for you. Failure to recognize the great worth of this recipe will cause you to miss a divine opportunity in your own life. It's easy for some to dismiss or minimize this formula because it consists of such common ingredients. Again, the value is not in the ingredients; it's in the recipe.

Today, the blessing of Abraham is a gift to all peoples everywhere. This formula was preserved for such a time as this. Mass, instant communication has ensured the ability to transmit human phenomena throughout the world instantly. Today, more than at any other time in history, humanity is in need of this powerful, elevating, transformational phenomenon. This formula is a critical instrument for navigating the maddening influences of a chaotic world in constant flux. The Creator intended for this sacred formula to provide man with divine elevation. You are encouraged to apply this extraordinary formula to your own life and, by exemplifying it, have a wonderful impact on the lives of others. You are now in possession of the royal family's treasure, the royal family's sacred formula.

2

THE GREATNESS OF YOUR FUTURE

Any doctrine presented to you as a means of liberation that does not bring you face-to-face with the *ultimate* version of *you* is incomplete at best, fraudulent at worst.

<u>MARRIED TO DEFEAT</u>

Many individuals are *married* to defeated identities. I'm not speaking literally of individuals married to other people. The individuals of whom I speak are committed to defeated self-concepts. They are yoked to defeated self-perceptions. Defeat is battering them in life, but they're in love with it. You may think you're helping them by showing them how to separate themselves from defeat, only to discover that you've gotten in the middle of a domestic dispute. Like most domestic disputes, outside intervention is dangerous. These individuals are not the least bit interested in victory. They're not prepared to leave their battering spouses. They don't want divorces. They have too much invested in their relationships. All their friendships and associations are based on their defeated identities. Defeat is all they know. Defeat, for them, is like a drug-addiction; like any other insidious addiction, the longer one is hooked, the more damage will occur. Self-destruction is the inevitable result.

An individual committed to defeat will cultivate a relationship with the Almighty in order to ensure entry into heaven upon death, but in the meantime wants to remain married to defeat right here on earth. His question of warning to others is, "What would become of you if you died today?" I would reverse the question. "What would become of you if you *lived* today?" Individuals committed to defeat don't even want victory right *now*; what makes them think they'll want it in heaven? They'll be trying to sneak out the backdoor of heaven to rendezvous with their real lover—in hell!

Many of us didn't need much prodding to separate from defeat. As soon as we were introduced to authentic victory, we were done with defeat. We immediately embraced victory. We had experienced so much pain, loss, tragedy, heartbreak, disappointment and sadness that all we needed was a divine alternative. All we needed was proper information.

TRUE VICTORY

A distinct glory accompanies the lives of the victorious. There's an aura surrounding them that bears witness to their personal blessing. This aura causes them to rise regardless of how low they are or how dire their situation, circumstance or environment. The victory within which they live makes them shine like lights. They have a dominant perspective of their own lives. Their lives produce victory because they *are* victorious already. They *are* a victory going somewhere to happen.

Personal identity is what distinguishes the victorious from the defeated. It's not whether an individual has won or lost in the past that determines victory or defeat in the present. It's not a matter of an individual's situation, circumstance or environment. It's not a matter of an individual's background or financial means. And it's not a matter of what others may think or say about him. Both victory and defeat are only and always a matter of present-tense self-concept.

An individual has either an identity of victory or an identity of defeat. Either way, a person's life will produce accordingly. True victory is only for those who must have it right now in this very moment. If you're not serious enough about victory to live in it right now, it's not for you. In fact, it will elude you, because it must. Remember the Law of Destiny. A tree must *be* an apple tree in order to produce apples. Likewise, a man must *be* victorious in order for his life to produce victory. Don't suppose you can postpone your victory. Postponed victory never comes; it cannot. If your victory is postponed, it's not victory that awaits you at all. Your life can only produce according to what you *already* are.

The sacred formula you've been introduced to in this text transforms lives by bringing individuals face-to-face with the *ultimate* versions of themselves, right here, right now, in this very moment. There are many phony representations of the genuine article on the market these days. Libraries, bookstores and other media are filled with various self-help philosophies and doctrines. The blessing of Abraham is not just a philosophy or a doctrine; it's a legacy—a divine human inheritance going back thousands of years. Human ultimacy is by far the most fascinating and effective transformational legacy of the human experience. The identity of victory extracted from your vision of victory but embraced in the present with absolute confidence is the genuine article. All other "knock-off" philosophies and doctrines are incomplete at best, fraudulent at worst.

Answering the Blessing Question was your personal treasure discovery. It was self-discovery at your highest level. What you've discovered isn't just *another* version of you; it's the *ultimate* version of you.

Notice the impact of ultimacy on the life of Jacob. His original name, which was indicative of the personal identity assigned to him at birth, means *supplanter*. He came to view himself as an illegitimate usurper, an imposter. This self-concept couldn't possibly produce the vision he was given for his life. But when he was exposed to the *ultimate* version of himself, *Israel*—a king with God—he compared the experience to seeing the face of God. He was moved so deeply by the experience that he named the geographical place of his revelation Peniel, which means, "the face of God."[13] This was the most significant turning point in Jacob's life. Jacob became *Israel*. To be sure, his twin brother Esau had a successful life, but he was never exposed to the ultimate version himself. His personal identity was sufficient, but not ultimate.

Let the discovery of your personal blessing—your identity of victory—be the most momentous event of your life, like seeing the face of God! To speak of self-realization is far too vague and abstract. After all, *degradation* is as real as ultimacy is. But if you're going to actualize anything in this life, actualize the *ultimate* version of you.

If you've already fully embraced your personal blessing as the truth about yourself in the present, you've already ordained true victory in your life. The outcome and quality of your living experience will be victorious because you *are* victorious already. You may not be accustomed to this kind of experience, so it may seem somewhat strange or peculiar. But you are exactly what you need to be *right now*. An internal change has already taken place. You are on the victory track right now. You've already been catapulted into another dimension of your life's reality. The Almighty wants you to live in this dimension at

---

13   GENESIS 32: 30

all times. He didn't create you to be minimized and degraded. You were created to be maximized and glorified. You're at your best when living in the inspiration of your own glory—in the inspiration of your own revealed greatness. Your personal blessing has propelled you into the glory of your destiny—in the present—where you must *remain*.

You have planted a particular kind of seed in the soil of your mind. That seed has already turned your life into a certain kind of tree. That tree is now in the process of reproducing the manner of fruit from which the seed came. Your life is now producing your vision. If you remain true to that identity, that identity will remain true to you in equal proportion. Cooperate fully with the process, and the process will cooperate with you.

Embracing your personal blessing was the best thing you ever did. The frame of mind you're now in isn't an exercise in futility. This phenomenon is taking you somewhere specific. It's so powerful that it's changing you in ways that transcend your conscious will. It's important to maintain an appreciation for what you've gotten into. When you began living wholeheartedly according to your personal blessing, you set in motion a revolutionary process. You're being uplifted, transformed and maximized *right now*, in this very moment. Never mind how things may appear, how things may look or seem outwardly. Never mind how contrarily others may be treating you right now. Outward contradictions are irrelevant. Being victorious, in spite of all else, is really all that matters. This is what it is to walk by faith and not by sight. You're living in great power right now, and you must realize it.

Your personal blessing has brought your inherited generational dysfunctions to a halt. Your personal blessing countervails all the madness of your present and past. The internal, unseen barriers that once hindered you have now been transcended. Everything inconsistent with your victorious identity is being eliminated systematically from your life. As you remain true, let it all go. Your personal blessing's polarity is rearranging your associations with everything and everyone. The most important thing you can now do is *remain* in the glorious spirit of your personal blessing at all times, with religious fervor. This is the challenge of your life. Your personal blessing has thrust you into the glory of your victorious future right now, in the present. Remain committed and watch the glory unfold before your eyes.

A NEW DIMENSION

Your identity of victory has altered your concept of what constitutes success for you. It has opened to you a completely new realm of reality. Your mind has been expanded. You're now looking beyond the psychological walls within which you were once bound. What is now normal for you is different than it was before. Things that once concerned you no longer do. Things you once focused on have been moved to the periphery. Your personal blessing has established a wonderful place for you, a high place for you. Your level of consciousness has risen to a new level, a level commensurate with the ultimate version of you. Your life is now following the blueprint of your personal blessing.

This experience is like moving into a luxury penthouse apartment that contains no furniture. You're the legitimate resident, true enough, but the décor doesn't yet reflect your presence. Don't be intimidated. Resist the temptation to vacate the premises. Resist the temptation to move back into the familiar due to any sort of personal insecurity. There is no reason to descend to where you were. Simply reclassify the elements of your life and settle in. This may prove uncomfortable for a time, but it's absolutely necessary. You're like Peter walking on water. This is a similar experience for you. Don't be dismayed by the raging winds. Don't look down and around in doubt. You have activated and are now operating in the most powerful dimension of your own being. Move confidently into your own greatness and remain there; this is the correct way for you to live.

TAKE YOURSELF SERIOUSLY

There are few things more tragic than a man who does not or cannot take himself seriously. Such a man can be bought, sold, intimidated and even seduced out of the glory of his own life. What is sad is that individuals aren't even conscious of how vulnerable they actually become when they don't take themselves seriously.

There are families who don't take their own children seriously. Individuals grow up in household environments where they were never taken seriously in any way. Their ability to take themselves seriously was never nurtured. They were never encouraged to take themselves seriously, nor was it ever implied that they were *worth* taking seriously. As these individuals grow into adulthood, they become unnaturally serious about menial, small things. Their natural instinct to be serious about something will cause them to be unnaturally serious about anything. They will express adult seriousness about childish things.

Among the things I appreciate most about the blessing phenomenon is that it reveals the most extraordinary identities to the most unlikely individuals and then requires them to take themselves seriously *immediately*. The blessing of Abraham reveals that the Almighty takes individuals far more seriously than they take themselves. He plays no games of gradualism or chance. He will not manifest extraordinary things through individuals who either will not or cannot take themselves seriously. He exposes individuals to the *ultimate* versions of them, and then in effect says, "Take yourself seriously right now! This is what you *are* right now; now get with the program so your life will produce accordingly!"

A powerful aura radiates from individuals who take themselves seriously. They have a focus that magnifies their objective. They have a personal discipline that keeps them within certain parameters. They have a relentless commitment that enables them to withstand vicious opposition but remain steadfast. Individuals who take themselves seriously stand out among those who do not. Individuals who take themselves seriously make things happen. Their personal identities compel their faculties without shame or intimidation. Throughout history, it has always been the individuals who took themselves seriously who brought about the most extraordinary achievements of the human experience. You need the focus, discipline and commitment that only come from taking yourself seriously. Without these attributes, you'll be deficient. You will lack in the most vital areas of your life. Take yourself seriously right now. What your personal blessing reveals is monumental in content; but it can only be realized by confidently taking yourself seriously.

Fortunately, your monumental manifestation doesn't rely upon others taking you seriously. If others *never* take you seriously, it's irrelevant to the ability of your life to produce according to your personal blessing's blueprint. Never allow the thoughts that others have toward you to alter your self-definition. The thoughts others have about *themselves* aren't even maximizing *their* lives. Their thoughts about *themselves* don't even serve *them* well. Why then should you take their thoughts regarding *you* into consideration in the least bit? The only thing that must be irrelevant in the mind of the victorious man is what others may think or say about him.

You're not headed for defeat or victory. You're either defeated or victorious right now; and what you are right now will determine the outcome and quality of your entire living experience. You don't have an appointment with victory; you have an appointment with destiny. You're victorious *already*. Your destiny simply reveals what you've been all along. Your victory is an experience, not an event. Your personal blessing *is* your victory. The greatness of your future is not *in* your future;

it's in *you* right now. The real treasure is not contained in where you're going; it's contained in what you're taking there. It's in what you *are* right now. It's in what your personal blessing has revealed about you.

Some have greater respect for where they're going than for what they are. This is a self-defeating way of operating. Your personal identity, *not your destiny*, is the most valuable, important and powerful aspect of your life. In fact, you'll forfeit your destiny of victory by diminishing your identity of victory. Your personal emphasis must always remain on *what* you are, because *that* is what actually produces your destiny.

"Arise, go thy way: thy faith hath made thee whole."[14] The identity aspect of the blessing phenomenon is the culmination of your faith. Abraham was the culminated faith of Abram. In the end, it wasn't enough for Abram to have a *hope*; it wasn't enough for him to *believe*; it wasn't enough for him to be *confident*; and it wasn't enough for him to be *faithful*. In the end, Abram required *Abraham*. Abraham was the centerpiece, the culmination and ultimate version of Abram. Without the reality of *Abraham*, the other dimensions of faith were powerless as it related to Abram's vision. *Abraham* was the seed that produced Abram's vision. *Abraham* contained the DNA, the specific genetic blueprint that could and would produce Abram's vision of victory. According to the story, Abram was already very rich; but he was unfulfilled. He was incomplete. *Abraham* is what made Abram whole, just as the ultimate version of you has made you whole. Now, rise up and go your way, for "thy faith hath made thee whole."

---

[14] LUKE 17:19

Your future isn't going to bring you greatness; you're going to bring greatness to your future. Your future is a neutral proposition, in that it's constrained to manifest what's planted in you, by you. What you *are* dictates the terms of your future. What you *are* is the seed that determines the product of your future. You must develop greater respect and reverence for what you *are,* in the present, despite how contradictory things may be or seem. The highest possible living experience available to you is always lived in the *present*, not the future. Your future will manifest the product of what you are right now. But the glory is not postponed. This is why it's better to be victorious in the midst of defeat than defeated in the midst of victory. It's better to be free in the midst of bondage than to be bound in the midst of freedom, because your life will always produce according to *what* you are and not *where* you are. What you are will always trump where you are. What you are will always transcend where you are. The power is in *what* you are, right here, right now, in this very moment. Never forget this.

THE NATURE OF YOUR RELATIONSHIPS

Throughout history, individuals have had interesting and intriguing relationships with themselves, others and their environments, particularly following dramatic changes in their personal identities. Who can fully understand human attraction and repellency? The people and things that attract at one stage of life are repelled at another, in no sure predictive pattern or sequence. The history of the blessing phenomenon bears witness to pronounced changes in the nature of the relationships of the blessed.

Isaac—believing he was conferring the blessing upon Esau—exhorted *Jacob* unknowingly, saying, "Let people serve thee, and nations bow down to thee . . ."[15] It was in fact this vision from which the identity of *Israel*, "a king with God," was later extracted. In effect, Isaac told Jacob that his relationship with the world had to change. Jacob, who was the least in his own family, ultimately became *Israel*, and had to "let" the nature of his relationships with everyone and everything change. He defined himself far higher than that to which he was accustomed. The history of his line reveals that his 12 sons became fathers of great tribes, separate family entities that would later grow into a great collective nation, which eventually came to constitute the basis of the highly exalted kingdom of biblical lore.

When lowly David, a youth at the time, received his personal blessing, he was forced to develop new relationships with everything and everyone: himself, the kingdom, the current king, the king's children, the royal servants, the soldiers, the royal citizens, women and even his enemies. David eventually came to terms with the fact that these changes, however awkward or painful, were *going* to happen. He realized that he had to *allow* them to happen. He eventually became king. Wearing the royal crown was far from roaming the hills tending to the sheep. His relationships with everyone and everything changed dramatically.

Long before David received his crown, he received his personal blessing through the prophet Samuel. His personal

---

[15]   GENESIS 27:29

blessing turned his life into a certain *kind* of tree; that tree produced according to what it was. David, however, had to be willing to allow the nature of his relationships with the world to change. His obedience in this regard set in motion the greatest royal legacy known to man.

Notice that when Yashua (the actual name of Jesus) went from operating in the identity of professional carpenter to the identity of messiah, the nature of all his relationships changed. His family members were the same. He even looked the same. He was the same individual. But the consciousness of his personal blessing changed the nature of the relationships he had with everything and everyone, including the nature of the relationship he had with himself. He now had a new full-time occupation. We have no record of Yashua strapped with a tool belt containing hammers, nails, measuring instruments and other items associated with the carpentry profession. We do however have record of activities indicative of the identity revealed by his personal blessing.

Following his baptism by John the Baptist, Yashua's destiny structure changed. His level of consciousness changed; his perspective changed; his agenda changed; his attitude changed; his aura changed; his words changed; his actions changed. The focus of his personal life changed, his personal priorities recalibrated. As a result, he acquired new friends and new enemies. He had to allow the nature of his relationships to change, and he did.

Even secular history bears witness to the effects of dramatic identity-change. Look at the history of Rome. Julius Caesar aimed to solidify the Republic of Rome into an empire. His relationships with everything and everyone changed when he suddenly went from operating in the identity of general to operating in the identity of emperor. The relationship Caesar had with himself was the first to change. After his army's fateful crossing of the Rubicon and the takeover that ensued, he laid aside his golden breastplate and donned instead a purple robe. He exchanged his gold-plated helmet for a wreath of leaves. His relationship with Rome changed. Instead of campaigning for it in the conquests of far off lands, he now ruled it. His relationship with the senate changed. He now *presided* over the very entity he once answered to, and refused to rise as the proud senators entered their hollowed chamber. His friends and enemies changed. In the end, it was a trusted friend—who was possibly his own son—to whom he famously uttered, "You too, Brutus?" as assassins' daggers pierced his flesh. The empire rose as Caesar fell.

When you embrace your personal blessing, the nature of the relationship you have with yourself will be the first to change. Self-abuse and self-neglect, if they ever existed in your life, will come to a halt. Your elevated self-concept will cause you to be more circumspect, more careful about yourself. It's not that you'll become timid, but self-consideration will cause you to think more deeply about yourself. The expectations you have of yourself will change. You'll see far-reaching implications in all that you are and do. There will be a dramatic restructuring of your priorities. Things that once meant nothing to you will now be top priority. Many things that once held high priority will be diminished greatly. Activities with which you once occupied yourself will be less important, and in some cases eliminated altogether. The demands you place on yourself will change. You'll find yourself inclined in directions you hadn't considered before. The points of emphasis in your life will change along with what you will allow of yourself. The pattern and trajectory of your behavior will change; your habits will change as your preparations for the future sharpen.

The relationship you have with yourself is important because it determines the nature of the relationships you have with everything and everyone else. Don't be alarmed, but the self-concept you've now moved into won't allow you to maintain some of your old relationships. Certain individuals will simply gravitate out of your orbit, because your polarity won't be what it once was. You won't have the same aura. You will attract a different caliber of individuals into your orbit. It's not an issue of richer or poorer, better or worse, but what once resonated with you simply won't anymore. What you once would accept, you won't anymore. You'll feed on a different kind of energy. Things that once impressed you no longer will. You'll vibe to a different kind of interaction. Who and what you're comfortable with will change. Individuals once drawn to you will be repelled; those once repelled now drawn. Enemies will become friends and friends will become enemies. Supporters will become detractors and detractors will become supporters. In fact, you won't really know who your friends or enemies are until you begin operating fully in your personal blessing.

Those drawn to or repelled from you are affected so by your identity of victory. The relationship others have with you is really a relationship with your personal blessing. When you begin to operate fully in the ultimate version of you, you'll experience a change in your perspective of others. Some of those you once looked up to will no longer hold that elevated position in your consciousness. It won't be that you somehow lost respect for them, but you'll simply view them from a different point of view. Those for whom you once had one-way admiration will begin to admire you. Those you once deferred to will now defer to you.

When you begin to operate fully in the greatness of your personal blessing, the nature of your relationships with the world outside will inevitably change. You'll develop different social parameters because you won't perceive life in the same way. Your situation, circumstance and environment won't necessarily change, but you'll view everything differently. The individuals in your environment won't necessarily change, but you'll view them all differently. For the first time you'll view everything and everyone from the *highest* perspective, which is the *proper* perspective from which to view your own life. You are what your personal blessing says you are; all else is relative.

Don't be intimidated by the changes in the nature of your relationships. The changes may seem strange, unfamiliar or even awkward. You should be mindful of a few things. First, these changes are *going* to occur; there are no ways around them. They are inevitable. Relationship changes come with the blessing territory. They need to occur and are a necessary aspect of the fulfillment of your destiny. You must allow these changes to occur. Don't stand in the way of what needs to happen; welcome the changes. The greatness of your future is within you *right now*, and you must not hesitate to experience the unfolding process, regardless of how your relationships may change during the process. No matter what, be true to the ultimate version of you.

3

ALL
YOU NEED
IS YOUR SEED

"It is like a grain of mustard seed, which, when it is sown in the earth, is less than all the seeds that be in the earth: But when it is sown, it groweth up, and becometh greater than all herbs, and shooteth out great branches; so that the fowls of the air may lodge under the shadow of it."[16]

[16] MARK 4:31-32

IDENTITY AS SEED

Developing a full appreciation for identity as seed has been a challenge for many ages. Even today, most are simply unaccustomed to viewing identity as seed. Once exposed to the blessing phenomenon, what remains is a major psychological adjustment with respect to the significance of your personal identity. Even Abram, in all his wisdom, couldn't figure out that what was inhibiting him was his own self-concept. Ultimately, manifesting his desired destiny wasn't an issue of physical ability or personal wealth; it was an issue of personal *identity*.

Most individuals have no difficulty respecting the power of *natural* seed. Even small children are taught early on how fruit seed works. They learn early to accept the fundamental principle that an apple seed is what produces an apple tree, which in turn produces apples. Parents understand how human seed works. Gardeners understand how garden seed works. Investors understand how financial seed works. The age-old challenge is to understand the concept of *identity* as seed.

If you have 10 thousand acres of land you want filled with apple trees, all you really need is one *single* apple seed. Though the seed is miniscule in size, it's mighty in potential. One tiny apple seed, which can fit on the tip of your finger, is powerful enough to fill 10 thousand acres or more with apple trees.

Likewise, if you have an extraordinarily immense vision for your life, all you really need is the tiny seed within it. The miniscule seed within the mighty vision is the *only* thing that can produce the vision. If you plant, feed and nurture the seed, it'll grow strong and multiply; but if you have no respect for it, you'll scorn and neglect it.

In order to prosper with this sacred formula, you must retrain your mind to respect your personal identity as a seed. Only then will you acknowledge your personal blessing as the amazing treasure it is, containing all your dreams, goals and aspirations. Only then will you make it the first, foremost and central focus of your life. Only then will you spend time with it, appreciating and cherishing it. Only then will you be focused on, committed to, and disciplined toward protecting it and bringing it to fruition. There is no true value in the definitions others have of you. The value is in your *self-assessment* based on your personal blessing. Your personal blessing is your greatest asset; it is your precious seed.

You must change your life's point of emphasis. It's all about *being* what your personal blessing has revealed about you. You have an extraordinary example to follow. "[L]ook unto the rock whence ye are hewn, and to the hole of the pit whence ye are digged. Look unto Abraham your father, and unto Sarah that bare you . . ."[17] The upshot of Abram's story is that he took *Abraham* seriously. He respected the power of the seed that was *Abraham*.

Abram came to realize that everything promised to him depended on him being *Abraham*—right now. He came to understand that he needed to *be* in order to become. Abram planted and nurtured the seed of *Abraham* in the soil of his own mind. This turned his life into that kind of tree. That tree

---

[17]   ISAIAH 51:1-2

had no choice but to produce the *fruit* determined by the seed. The miracle birth of Isaac was the result.

For decades, Abram and Sarai performed the physical act that would eventually produce Isaac, but to no avail. The act, in and of itself, lacked the power necessary to produce the extraordinary results they wanted, because the identities within which the *act* took place were *not* extraordinary. Abraham and Sarah were extraordinary identities; Abram and Sarai were *ordinary* identities. Abraham and Sarah constituted precious seed, the *only* seed that could produce their extraordinary dream. Your personal blessing is also precious seed, and you should respect it as such.

RIPEN YOUR VISION

It is my purpose in this work to assist you in the discovery of your personal blessing. I must emphasize, however, that it is in fact *your* discovery. It's also my purpose to provide you with information that will increase your understanding *following* your discovery. I do have boundaries and rules I must abide by in my endeavor. For instance, I cannot declare unto you what your personal blessing should or shouldn't be. Such a matter is strictly between you and the Creator of us all. I *can* tell you that your personal blessing derives from the glorious vision the Almighty has given to you for your life. I am merely an executor of the *blessing estate*. What you discover and what you do with that discovery is beyond my purview. My job is to make sure you have *access* to the information that brings you face-to-face with your personal treasure.

There are extraordinary things within you that defy what anyone else can possibly imagine for you. Anyone's attempt to define you in victorious terms may in fact minimize you. The most I could've told the Wright Brothers was that they were the best bicycle makers in the world. This is the most I would've been able to perceive in them. This assessment may have *sounded* elevating, but would've been degrading. As it turned out, the Creator placed something *within* them that defied what anyone else could've possibly imagined *for* them. They possessed something greater than anyone else could've possibly known. Propelled flight was a far more advanced human development than an improved bicycle.

The key word in the Blessing Question is *vision*. Your vision for your life is your *hope*. Hope is a necessity of life. Your personal blessing is extracted from your hope. Remember, the culmination of your faith is the identity of victory extracted from your vision of victory—extracted from your *hope*. Your identity of victory is nothing but a seed, the very substance of the thing you're *hoping* for, the evidence of the thing not yet seen. Seed bears witness to the fruit it comes from, but if you have no hope—no vision for the future—you have nothing from which to extract your victorious seed. You can have no culminated faith without a hope. As in a prosecutorial court proceeding, if you have no evidence, you can't make your case. The vital element of the blessing phenomenon is your hope, that is, your *vision of your victorious future*. This is particularly true if you've experienced great loss, trauma or some sort of great deprivation. Following such an experience, the ability to embrace your personal blessing may be especially challenging, because traumatic experiences strike directly at your hope. The one thing you must always maintain is your hope, a vision of your victorious future. Never give it up. As the Rev. Jesse L. Jackson Sr. is known for proclaiming, "Keep hope alive!" Your ability to keep your hope alive can be a matter of life and death. Your hope will sustain you until your seed extraction takes place. It will even sustain you following the planting process. "For there is hope of a tree, if it be cut down, that it will sprout again . . . through the scent of water it will bud, and bring forth boughs like a plant."[18]

Hope sustained Abram for years. He eventually received the greatness of Abraham. Hope sustained Sarai for years. She eventually received the greatness of Sarah. Hope sustained Jacob for years. He eventually received the greatness of Israel. Hope sustained Joseph, son of Jacob, for years. He eventually received the greatness of Zaphnath-paaneah—*"revealer of secret things, prince of the life of the Age"*[19]—his elevated personal identity as ruler in Egypt. It was Joseph's *hope* that sustained him through the trauma of false imprisonment and the psychological challenges thereto appertaining.

Your hope, your vision of victory, is like the fruit of a tree. Fruit doesn't start out clear, distinctive and complete. It develops through a ripening process. The ripening of a vision, like the ripening of fruit, is a process. A vision of victory may take a few moments to develop or it may require years. Whatever the

---

[18]   JOB 14: 7, 9
[19]   GENESIS 41:45

case, the development of your personal vision is a *process*, and is vital to the blessing phenomenon.

One important fact to bear in mind is that the seed within fruit ripens along with the fruit. If the fruit is unripened, the seed within it will have no power; it will be impotent due to underdevelopment. A seed is only as potent as the fruit is mature. Potent is the root word of potential. The potential of a seed correlates directly with the ripeness of the fruit from which it derives. As anyone will attest, unripened fruit doesn't taste as good as ripened fruit. You're not driven to the core of fruit that doesn't taste good. In fact, you'll struggle with the very first bite. Conversely, you're driven easily to the core of fruit that is appealing to the taste. This is divine design, for it is at the core of the apple where you'll find the seed that can reproduce it. The core contains the treasure freely given to those who have *first* appreciated the taste. Ripened fruit compels the eater to the core. Ripened fruit beckons the eater to the seed within it. The same dynamic applies to *your* hope—your vision of victory.

Your vision of victory and your identity of victory ripen contemporaneously, that is, at the same time. As with any other seed, there is a direct correlation between the maturity of the vision and the potency of the corresponding identity. An unripened vision cannot provide you with the powerful identity that can produce it. If your vision isn't clear, detailed and complete, neither will be the identity extracted from it. If your vision of victory hasn't ripened, your identity of victory will be powerless. In fact, you'll struggle to arrive at it. If, on the other hand, your vision is clear, detailed and complete, the identity within it will potent in equal proportion.

If you're struggling to arrive at your personal blessing, ripen your vision. The only way to receive an effective identity of victory from your vision of victory is to *ripen* your vision. Make your vision clear, vivid and graphic in your own mind. Make your vision detailed, specific and precise in your own mind. Make your vision mature, complete and whole in your own mind. Put your vision into words, which will help you capture the essence of what your vision of victory is really about. "Write the vision, and make it plain upon tables, that he may run that readeth it."[20] This facilitates your ability to arrive at the core of your vision, where you will inevitably find your personal blessing. Your answers to the Blessing Question will flow if you'll only ripen your vision. This is important because your vision of victory reveals extraordinary things about you—*to you*.

THE BIGGER PICTURE

There is a bigger picture of you. You must be willing to open your eyes to it. Boldly take it all in and accept the findings. You must actively participate in this process. Turn on the light of your soul and let your inner eyes adjust. Don't settle for a partial view of yourself. Don't settle for a limited view of yourself. You are great, multi-dimensional and monumental. You're a giant among men, past, present and future. If no one else ever sees this in you, that's fine. You're the only person who *needs* to view you like this in order for it to work.

---

[20] HABAKKUK 2:2

When this phenomenon was first introduced to Abram, what the Almighty revealed to him was far greater than he previously knew. In effect, God said to Abram, "You're too small in your own sight. You need to be bigger in your own sight. You're experiencing your life beneath yourself. Your low self-estimation is inhibiting your life. You're a giant among men. You're *Abraham*, father of many nations right now; now wrap your mind around that and get with the program!" Abram needed exposure to the bigger picture of himself.

Many are afraid of a larger, grander inner-image of themselves. They worry how they'll appear if they fully conformed to the ultimate versions of themselves. They're unwilling to step out of their social and psychological comfort zones. They worry about whose sensibilities they may offend. But I say to you, imagine all those who would be offended if you operated fully within the ultimate version of yourself. Offend them, I say! If living triumphantly in your personal blessing offends the expectations or sensibilities of others, I say to you, let them be offended. You cannot sacrifice the precious moments of your life to satisfy or reconcile the lowly assessments others have of you. Be willing to open your eyes, remove your blinders and accept the full glory of the *ultimate* version of you right here, right now, in this very moment. This is what the blessing formula entails.

When you were exposed to your personal blessing, you were in effect invited into a great and glorious life—nothing less. It doesn't matter how low you may have sunk into the mire of life. Your personal blessing will lift you up and out of that madness. This is what its genetic blueprint is designed and constrained to do. Exaltation is in the DNA of your personal blessing. This is why it's so important for you to be exposed to the bigger picture of you. This is why ripening your vision is so crucial. Planting and nurturing your personal blessing will empower you up and out of *any* circumstance. It will be true to you if you will be true to it.

Conform only to your personal blessing. Realize this process is going to expose things about you, to you, that you did not know. Be willing to both acknowledge and operate fully in those high truths. They were revealed to you for a reason. Accept the *ultimate* version of you. Humble yourself to it. Be obedient to it. Your personal blessing has given you a glorious path to follow. It's given you a new life to live. Don't be afraid of your own glorious seed. Don't be afraid of the bigger picture of you. To live any other way is rebellion against the divine purpose for your life; it is *sin*.

Falling into self-intimidation can be easy. As we discussed earlier, the force of personal identity is very powerful. Personal identity is the operational program of your life. Personal identity has the ability to sweep you into another dimension *of* life. Personal identity is what directs your life. It's therefore no surprise that your identity of victory, the *ultimate* version of you, can be daunting. The revealed picture of the ultimate version of you may be larger and more extraordinary than you were prepared to realize or grasp. It's so much more convenient to accept a narrow, constricted version of yourself. Personal ultimacy can be so overwhelming that it can actually make you call a "time out." In sports, "time outs" are breaks in the action used strategically to regroup or to recalibrate. You may need some time to get yourself together following exposure to your personal blessing. You may need time to consider thyself, to take it all in, mentally and emotionally.

The most dramatic event in any man's life is when he's exposed to the *ultimate* version of himself. This personal exposure of oneself *to* oneself can even be an emotional event. You'll realize for the first time that what the Almighty thinks of you is so much greater than what you thought of yourself. You'll realize how the world has worked to cheapen, minimize and degrade you. But you'll also realize how you've actually *participated* in cheapening, minimizing and degrading yourself. You've unwittingly played the chump role in your own life. You've played the pawn role in the chess game of your own life.

You're greater than you actually knew. Live in this greatness and shine with the glory of your personal blessing for the rest of your life. This is the correct way for you to live. Don't let it be said that you were greater than you were willing to accept. You may understandably experience a degree of blessing-shock. After all, your personal blessing is astonishingly revealing. The answers you provided to the Blessing Question represent the various dimensions of your personal blessing, the *highest* version of you. Not only will others understandably struggle to classify you, but you also may struggle to classify yourself.

Even King David was moved to ask, "Who am I, O Lord God, and what is mine house, that thou hast brought me hitherto?"[21] King David's personal blessing challenged his human capacity to receive it, but receive it he did. He was already bigger than life, in that he was king of a profound

---

[21] I CHRONICLES 17:16

kingdom. But as time proceeded, he was exposed to an even larger picture of himself. He had to come to terms with the fact that he was much greater, far more extraordinary, than he previously knew. He was a giant among men, not in personal stature, but in scope of consciousness. He came to terms with his own greatness and accepted it. He would go on to establish fully Yahweh's (God's) Kingdom in the land of promise. He would also establish an everlasting royal lineage, a royal legacy that continues to have an extraordinary impact on the lives of billions, as it has throughout the centuries.

There is more to any identity than meets the eye. An identity is like an iceberg, most of it submerged beneath the surface. Any identity is like an island, a great mountaintop piercing the midst of the sea. Most of what actually exists is out of sight; that which is above the surface merely bearing witness to a greater portion. There is more to being a husband and father than is apparent on the surface, more to being a wife and mother than is apparent on the surface. Living in any identity will progressively result in greater self-realization. There are aspects and dimensions of life that can only be revealed by continuously and consistently living in a particular identity. Only in time is a clearer perception of your role, position and responsibilities revealed.

The longer you remain in a particular identity, the more will be revealed about it—to you. The cycle of any personal identity lasts a lifetime, however long or short. Over a span of a lifetime things become clearer and are better understood. This is also the case with the identity revealed by your personal blessing. You'll realize that you are far greater than you thought you were. This realization will crystallize as time proceeds. The truth is that you are more special, more significant and more wonderful than you can fully grasp at this moment. In the fullness of time, though, you'll increasingly develop more respect for yourself. You'll experience a continual internal metamorphosis enduring your lifetime. Prepare yourself mentally to live it out for the long haul. It's well worth it. There is more to you than you realize. You've not yet seen the greater part of yourself. Embracing your personal blessing was just the beginning, the catalyst of an extraordinary living experience. What's important is that you remain faithful to your identity of victory, to the best of your ability, at all times.

Your personal blessing is a living organism. There will be many wonderful outgrowths and manifestations that you can't possibly anticipate stemming from your personal blessing. Though the way may seem strange, things will only get better for you. Endure the test of time and watch your life produce a level of greatness even you couldn't have imagined. "Eye hath not seen, nor ear heard, neither have entered into the heart of man, the things which God hath prepared for them that love him."[22] Your personal blessing is actually more glorious than you have the capacity to comprehend at present. Incrementally, the glory will be revealed to you. But you have exactly what you need. All you need is your seed. Be true to it and it will be true to you.

---

[22]   I CORINTHIANS 2:9

4

YOU ARE AMAZING!

You're not headed for defeat or victory; you're either defeated or victorious right now, and what you are right now will determine the outcome and quality of your entire living experience.

DOCTRINAL CAPTIVITY

For ages, man has searched for the keys that unlock the great mysteries of life. From the ancient temple-colleges of the Nubians along the Nile River to the flowering of eastern thought in India, man has attempted to answer the great and eternal questions surrounding human nature. From the Golden Ages of the Greeks and Romans to the European Renaissance and Age of Enlightenment, man has postulated and proposed answers to the mysteries surrounding the human experience. To this end, man has developed countless doctrines, religions and philosophies.

The minds of multitudes are held captive by doctrinal, religious and philosophical positions influential individuals have spawned throughout the millennia. In some cases, peoples have been virtually *locked* into stifling, inhibiting doctrines for thousands of years. Some of these doctrines assert that man should seek to *eliminate* his individuality in deference to some arbitrary group identity. Some assert that man has no control over his personal destiny and should therefore yield it to arbitrary forces. Others assert that outward actions, choices and decisions are the sources of destiny. Still others assert that outward actions, choices and decisions are the sources of identity. Some doctrines even assign personal identities to individuals based on their dates of birth or to the caste into which they were born. Given the advent of modern technology, there have even been efforts to pin down personal identity based on blood type. There are many such twisted belief systems and pseudo sciences throughout the world today.

The problem, of course, is that individuals born into societies dominated by such doctrines and belief systems are *deprived* of the divine option revealed by the Law of Human Nature. One cannot consciously choose his date of birth or his caste, much less his own blood type. So in effect, multitudes have been born into *captivity*. Peoples have been born into limiting doctrines brought forth and left behind by, presumably, the luminaries of their respective times. But are there any other societies upon the earth noted for the propagation of the blessing formula? Has such a society ever existed before now? If so, when and where? Because if such a society *ever* existed, it would *be* here now!

I'm not oblivious to the fact that many have had the wherewithal to throw off the chains into which they were born. Many have embraced doctrines and belief systems of their own choosing. But from what selection did they choose? What were their choices? I would ask these individuals several questions. First, when you selected your belief system, what exactly were you looking for? Did you find what you were looking for or did you simply settle for something? Were you running to a battle or from one? Were you so adamant about getting away from what you had known that it didn't really matter what you stumbled upon, so long as it was different from that which you were abandoning? In arriving at your personal belief system, were you pursuing some solution or simply running from a problem, or both?

This line of questioning begs an even more comprehensive question. Namely, what should be the ultimate aim of any human doctrine as it relates to life on earth? Is it social control, morality, the greatest good for the most people or what? We now know that the effect any belief system has upon individuals depends largely on the motives of those teaching it. History reveals that wonderful doctrines can be used for nefarious purposes. With this in mind, when a man is introduced to a particular belief system, he should ask no less than three questions. Why are you introducing me to *this* doctrine? What is *your* interest in teaching me this doctrine? If I were to embrace this doctrine, what would become of my life on earth, right here, right now, in this very moment? Why are these questions important? The answer is obvious.

A lifetime on earth consists of precious *moments*. Individuals need to be exposed to the *highest* possible living experience available to them—right here, right now, in this *very* moment. Life is far too short and precious for anything less. The irrepressible march of time is the common denominator of all life on earth. This is why the very moments of time must be maximized. What good is a doctrine for living that promises a pie-in-the-sky after you die, but completely misses the mark when it comes to the outcome and quality of your living experience right here on earth, in this very moment in time?

Think of wild animals raised in captivity, trained from birth to comply with the whims of man. Humans rake in large sums of money from the exotic tricks these animals are taught to perform. Tigers jump through fiery hoops. Elephants do headstands. Killer whales play beach-ball games. Occasionally, though, these animals snap into violent rages, perhaps experiencing genetic flashbacks of some sort. It seems that in spite of all the intensive training and behavior reinforcement, the God-ordained nature of the animal still exists. The human condition is akin to these examples in one interesting way.

While humans are certainly not wild animals, they *are* indoctrinated into stifling, limiting systems of thought and behavior. They *are* indoctrinated into compliance with unjust social orders, negative stereotypes and destructive behavior. Humans *are* indoctrinated into slavery, second-class citizenship, vagabondage, war and even self-destruction. Humans *are* indoctrinated into hate; to the extent, they become complicit in genocide and other heinous crimes against humanity. In short, humans *are* indoctrinated into any number of lifestyles and ways of thinking by the systematized propaganda of *others*.

Now and then, though, a man will experience a glimpse, a flash of another version of himself. A man will experience an epiphany, a sublime window through which he can see a version of himself he has never fully experienced. It's at these moments that a man is most prone to rebel against stifling, hindering factors. He may not even understand his rebellion, but his God-given instincts reveal to him that something is amiss in his life; that there is more to him than he's actually experiencing. It is for this cause that the blessing formula exists.

The differences in human theologies reflect the various dimensions of reality to which individuals and groups are bearing witness. The blessing of Abraham provides man with an epiphanous foundation upon which to build his life. It enables man to experience himself on the most glorious level by bringing him face-to-face with the *ultimate* version of himself. It serves as a comprehensive catalyst for extraordinary, dramatic personal transformation. The blessing formula is undoubtedly human liberation at the *highest* level.

By far, the greatest introduction of my life was to the ultimate version of me: **the Prophet of this Millennium.** I had never formally been introduced to this version of me. To be sure, I'd caught glimpses of this version through the years, but I could never really capture the essence of all that it was until I ripened my vision and answered the Blessing Question honestly. As it turned out, the *ultimate* version of me was extraordinary, far higher and greater than that which I had previously known. I haven't been the same since. This text is the fruit of my personal blessing. "[T]he tree is known by his fruit . . . A good man out of the good treasure of the heart bringeth forth good things: and an evil man out of the evil treasure bringeth forth evil things."[23]

Why is the discovery of the ultimate version of *you* so important? There are two primary reasons. First, if you never come to know the ultimate version of you, then you can't introduce him to anyone or anything else. Those who have a right to know him and to bask in his glory will never get those opportunities. Second, if you don't embrace the ultimate version of you, you'll forfeit the highest possible living experience available to you. You'll forfeit the highest possible level of freedom and liberation available to you. Instead of experiencing ultimacy in the precious moments of your life, those moments will be degraded and wasted in mediocrity, or worse.

Any doctrine presented to you as a systematized method of personal liberation that doesn't bring you face-to-face with

---

[23] MATTHEW 12:33, 35

the *ultimate* version of you is incomplete at best, fraudulent at worst. Such a doctrine actually *condemns* you to what some other person upon the earth *settled* for at some point in history. Indeed, that person may have had *some* type of spiritual awakening or experience, but was it the *ultimate* spiritual awakening or experience? If not, why would you commit *your* life to it? Should your life be condemned to the parameters of another man's limited experience? It doesn't matter who or what they claim or claimed to be. If their doctrine did not pointedly introduce *you* to the ultimate version of *you* as a unique individual right here, right now, in this very moment, what have they really done *for* you—or, more specifically, *to* you? I'm just asking. What is more insidious than holy sounding fraudulence shrouded in the rhetoric and mysticism of liberating religiosity? Away with such madness! *Ultimacy* is what life on earth is all about.

"[G]lory, honour, and peace, to every man that worketh good . . ."[24] You're *entitled* to "glory, honour, and peace" right here, right now, in this very moment. Beware of being bought-off cheaply. Limiting doctrines deprive you of a maximized life; they seduce you into mediocrity. They tease you with ambiguity. They rob you of the sacredness of your precious moments. They deny you the treasure of your own wonderful life, *selling* you nuggets to your treasure, when they should just give you the key to the door while moving out of the way. They hit the target but miss the bull's-eye, then ask you to celebrate their "victory" with *your* life. But don't do it. Don't settle for less. Don't be seduced into mediocrity. There is

---

[24]   ROMANS 2:10

an unknown, unrealized version of you within your vision of victory. There is a structure of greatness within your personal blessing. Follow the course of this structure. This is the most you can do, but it's all that you *need* to do. Throw off your chains immediately, and be true to the *ultimate* version of you. Be free right now!

What's wonderful about the Almighty is that He doesn't need permission from others to expose you to the highest version of you. He doesn't require someone else's limited understanding to validate the blossoming of your personal living experience. He doesn't require corresponding forces or some arbitrary confluence of events; He doesn't require a majority vote; He exposes you at His own discretion, despite any other factors that may or may not be at play in your midst. You don't have to be anyone else's favorite in order to garner the favor of the Almighty.

Today I view the panoply of "liberating" doctrines, philosophies and religions in a new light. The blessing of Abraham provides a standard against which to measure the efficacy and legitimacy of the various positions staked out by others throughout the course of the human experience. If I could ask the founders and propagators of these doctrines pointed questions, they would be along the lines of: "When were you going to get around to bringing me face-to-face with the *ultimate* version of me, as a unique individual, in this very moment?" "Were you going to condemn me to living like a trained animal, jumping through hoops and performing degrading tricks forever?" "Why do you expect me to commit my life to celebrating you hitting the target but missing the bull's-eye?"

The precious moments of your life are too valuable to commit them to someone else's limited experience—to someone else's mediocrity. Some doctrines are based more on increasing group membership than in activating greatness within the individual. Some seek to pacify adherents with hollow encouragement. The problem with these "rah-rah-you-can-do-it" theologies is that adherents are bought-off cheaply by a fleeting rush of emotional adrenaline. Adherents are merely pacified, their state of personal degradation anesthetized. These individuals are seduced by charismatic smooth-talk. No victorious destiny structure is provided by these kinds of doctrines. Individuals are sent afloat, wishing, hoping aimlessly in a pond without a rudder, sure to wash up on some nearby bank.

Some doctrines urge adherents to control their actions or to focus on the goal itself. Others correctly teach adherents to believe they receive, but never place emphasis squarely on personal redefinition. Some doctrines restrict individuals to "the common faith,"[25] but wholly neglect *personal faith*. These doctrines restrict the lives of individuals to "cookie-cutter" spiritual and personal identities, as if somehow the Almighty is unable to do anything profound and unique in the lives of individuals in this day and time.

Self-redefinition in accordance with a vision of victory is what actually triggers the process that manifests extraordinary supernatural things right here on earth. What searching individuals really need to know is that destiny-control stems from

---

[25] TITUS 1:4

identity-control. If you have limited control of your personal identity, you will correspondingly have limited control of your personal destiny. You'll be tossed about by the ever-changing winds of situations, circumstances, environments, events and the arbitrary projections of others.

There are doctrines that teach adherents to pray and "just let God do it," when it comes to the manifestation of your vision. Ostensibly, if God *won't* do it for you, it wasn't meant to be. The problem with this teaching is that God already did it! He set the system in motion at the beginning of time. Recognize though that you're an active participant in the process of your destiny. Everything you require is already within you, right now. "[B]ehold, the kingdom of God is within you."[26] The butterfly is already in the caterpillar. The orchard is already in the seed. Your victory is already in you because your identity of victory *came* from your vision of victory.

A man and a woman's children are already within them. They may petition the Almighty for a baby. They may pray, fast and bring their gift to the altar; but if they don't plant the seed already in their possession, they will never conceive. They are the most active participants in the process. It's not that God won't grant their petition. He has already granted their heart's desire. What they're asking for is already within them. God governs seasons, but individuals govern their own seed.

A farmer can pray for a harvest, but if he never plants any seed, there can be no harvest. The farmer is an active participant in the manifestation of his vision. God isn't responsible for the farmer's inability to reap a harvest. The Almighty made sure

---

[26] LUKE 17:21

that planting *and* harvest seasons came. But because the farmer planted no seed, he was unable to reap any harvest.

The Almighty is in control of the seasons, but you are always in control of your personal seed. Remember, an identity is nothing but a seed. There is no reason to be intimidated by the nature of your extraordinary identity. It's just a seed, albeit the *only* seed that can produce your extraordinary vision.

What I've discovered to be the sad truth is that others will stand by and *watch* you live beneath yourself. Some actually want you to live beneath yourself. Some *need* you to live beneath yourself; they *benefit* when you live beneath yourself. There are entities that have an interest in a degraded version of you. If you experienced full and complete liberation in this very moment, there would be no need or use for what they represent.

There are predatory, vulturous elements that actually benefit from human captivity and destruction. There are *official* entities in certain societies that perversely benefit from crime and criminals. Some societies have legalized the operation of corporate penal institutions—*privatized prisons*—whose financial bottom lines depend on human captivity. It costs government less to incarcerate humans in these corporately owned prisons than in government-run facilities. Financially incentivizing locking people up has resulted in officially sanctioned social cannibalism at a rate not seen since slavery. Now, lobbyists representing the financial interests of prison corporations routinely petition government to criminalize everything conceivable in order to create policing practices conducive to their clients' interests. They need bodies in jail. They press for vigorous and intensive law enforcement targeting the young and poor. Their livelihoods depend on skyrocketing crime statistics and burgeoning prison populations. Even judges, police officers, public defenders and prosecutors in these societies buy stock in corporate prisons. In carrying out their everyday duties, these individuals ensure maximum financial compensation by vigorously incarcerating the most vulnerable members of society. The primary justification provided for building prisons today is not to house dangerous criminals, but to provide much needed *employment* in economically hard-hit areas.

I point this out to underscore the urgency with which a man must embrace the *ultimate* version of himself. There are vicious predatory interests poised against him already. There's no need for him to join the ranks of his own opposition by minimizing *himself*, becoming even more vulnerable.

AUTHENTIC TRANSFORMATION

I encourage you to move into another direction of understanding, into another dimension of conscious reality. Introduce yourself to the *ultimate* version of you and be *one* with it. Your answer to the Blessing Question is a seed. Plant that seed. Embrace your answer right now, with absolute confidence. Shine with the glory of your identity of victory. Shake off any shame or apprehension. That version of you *is* you; it's the *ultimate* version of you; the *highest* version of you; the *greatest* version of you. Develop an appreciation for the most wonderful version of *you*. You will transform in ways that are so profound that you won't even realize when many of the changes within you occur.

Look at the example of the caterpillar. In order for the caterpillar to transform into a butterfly, it must only remain true to itself. In a sense, the caterpillar is the seed of the butterfly. It already contains the DNA, the genetic blueprint of what it *will* become. The destiny structure that will produce the highest possible level of freedom and liberation, the highest possible living experience available to the caterpillar, is already within it. Being true to what it is at one stage of its life, despite the lowly appearance of things, *activates* the reality of its experience at another stage of its life. There is a process, a method to this type of transformation. If the caterpillar attempts to jump into flight from some high point, it risks serious injury or worse. But if it remains true to what it is, it will experience that which will enable it to thrive. Such is the case with you.

There's a hidden process in *being* that is only experienced *by* being. You can only experience it by being true to what you are, inwardly. As mentioned earlier, true transformation isn't about becoming in order to be; it's about *being* in order to become. What's the process by which a caterpillar is able to fly? It obviously needs wings, but the mystery of the cocoon is revealed only as the caterpillar remains true to what it is.

The caterpillar doesn't have to manufacture wings; its *life* will produce them. Its transformation isn't in creative outward escapades or any other seemingly obvious activity, but by a means just the opposite. *Being* reveals a process that isn't so obvious. As it turns out, the liberation of the caterpillar comes through a process of dark seclusion and isolation. The process that provides wings for the caterpillar defies any logical, well thought-out obvious action on its part. The mystery of becoming is wrapped up in the obscure glory of *being*. The authenticity associated with *being* is what provides the caterpillar with its ultimate grandeur.

Being something in particular enables one to become something in particular. The commitment, though, is to *being*. The greatness, power and glory of your life are experienced through *being*. Your personal process of transformation is only revealed to you through *being*. The mysteries, the unknowable phases of your victorious experience, are only activated by *being*. Your cocoon phase, whatever it is for you, is only experienced through *being*. Attempted action, absent the unique experience of *being* is ineffective and inauthentic. It's like trying to fly without wings, or the absurd equivalent of a caterpillar trying to manufacture wings or leaping into dangerous descending flight; correct idea, wrong method. There will come a time when you won't even be able to crawl anymore, but you must remain absolutely true to what you are *right now* in order to move into that phase. *Being* reveals things to you that you can't possibly figure out on your own.

"To every thing there is a season, and a time to every purpose under heaven . . ."[27] Life is seasonal. It's important to experience every season of your living process while operating fully in your personal blessing. Live truly through all seasons, at all times, and not randomly or arbitrarily. Seasons have a job to perform. They create the stage for your emergence. They create the conditions necessary for the manifestation of your vision.

---

[27] ECCLESIASTES 3:1

Seasons, however, are not in your control. Times change, and things change in time. Your life is lived against the backdrop of alternating seasons. Playing yourself falsely at any time can cause you to miss your critical season. Your personal blessing is not a jacket to be put on or off depending on the weather; it's not a light-switch to be turned on or off as needs arise.

"He that observeth the wind shall not sow; and he that regardeth the clouds shall not reap."[28] Missing your season can never be attributed to what you didn't do, but to failing to be true—true to the *ultimate* version of you. When you're not true, your life's timing is thrown out of calibration. Your season of opportunity comes and goes while you are indecisively straddling the fence of your personal reality. There are opportunities that can only be seized while living in your personal blessing. You'll only perceive them *as* opportunities while operating in the ultimate version of you. Operating outside your identity of victory will cause you to miss clear and present opportunities. The glow of your personal blessing is what reveals your opportunities to you. You'll miss wide open doors when you're not shining true. You won't see what you should've seen; you won't hear what you should've heard; you won't perceive what you should've perceived. And you won't think what you should've thought. The conditions were true, but you were not.

There are personal phases and changes that accompany every season of your experience. These internal phases and changes are critical to the manifestation of your destiny. When you're not 100 percent true to your blessing experience, the

---

[28]   ECCLESIASTES 11:4

continuity of your process is broken and your blessing instincts are blunted. You'll be speaking when you should be silent and silent when you should be speaking. You'll be moving when you should be still and still when you should be moving. You'll be absent when you should be present and present when you should be absent. You'll be connecting when you should be detaching and detaching when you should be connecting. You'll be laughing when you should be crying and crying when you should be laughing.

Your destiny is not a manufactured product; it is produced organically through your life. It's an authentic manifestation of your living experience. The transition of your position comes from remaining true, not from what you do. It's impossible to understand fully everything you're experiencing right now; it cannot be understood completely. Further along your path, though, you'll know more about it. A faithful experience doesn't provide a full understanding during the experience itself, but it's only a matter of time until your faithful experience provides you with the wings required to fulfill your destiny.

What actually constitutes victory in your life? Winning for those of us in possession of the blessing formula is different than it is for others. *We're* winning when we operate in our identities of victory, our personal blessings. While living wholeheartedly in the *ultimate* versions of ourselves, we *are* victorious, because we're experiencing the highest possible level of freedom and liberation available to us, right here, right now, in this very moment.

Never mind how things look, appear or seem. All contradictory outward appearances are irrelevant. You must be willing to shine in your victorious identity in the midst of what may appear to be a losing situation, circumstance or environment. It's better to be victorious in the midst of defeat than to be defeated in the midst of victory, because your life will always produce according to *what* you are and not where you are. What you are always transcends where you are. Despite the way things may appear, you are winning as long as you're operating fully in your personal blessing.

Victory requires audacity. You must be bold and audacious when it comes to being what your personal blessing has revealed. The blessing of Abraham is not a gradualist phenomenon. When you received your personal blessing, it propelled you into another dimension of reality. This dimension isn't for the faint of heart or the weak of mind. The process requires mental strength, personal tenacity and fortitude. Enduring the experience of *being* is what earns the fulfillment of your dream. Your willingness to shine with the glory of your identity of victory in the midst of surrounding darkness is vital. The most challenging thing you'll ever endure is your *own* glory. But it's a necessary endurance. If you can't handle being, you can't handle what being produces. If you can't handle the identity, you can't handle the destiny.

Your victory is not an event; it's an *experience*. The experience of victory is what produces the fulfillment of your vision. The sprouting of apples isn't the apple tree's victory. The sprouting of apples is the fulfillment of the tree's victorious *experience*. The tree has lived through multiple barren seasons and has been victorious and true to itself through them all. A championship is the culmination of a championship season. It's the fulfillment of a championship *experience*. The reason your life is producing a personal championship for you right now is because you are a champion already—inwardly. You think like a champion—already. You view things from a champion's perspective—already. You have the agenda of a champion—already. You have the attitude of a champion—already. You have the aura of a champion—already. You speak the words of a champion—already. You act like a champion—already. You live like a champion—already. You function with the discipline of a champion in your preparation and in your lifestyle—already. Your life has no choice but to produce a championship, because you *are* a champion—already.

Even your personal losses, injuries and penalties are vital parts of your championship experience. Acknowledging and correcting your human frailties, faults and shortcomings are significant parts of your championship experience. Your disappointments and mistakes are as much parts of your championship experience as are the crowning ceremonies themselves.

BLESSING BENEFICIARIES

Others need exposure to your victorious experience. When you shine, others are inspired to shine as well. In this way, your personal blessing is like divine contagion. It's a catalyst for victory in the lives of others. Your victorious experience is like the assemblage of a thousand-piece puzzle. In the assembly, clusters of pieces always form. These clusters constitute the nuclei of what will eventually be a complete picture. You are like a cluster of puzzle-pieces. A complete picture is being assembled around you. You are the light of the world and the salt of the earth when you're operating in your personal blessing. Like the sun, you represent the centerpiece of a dynamic human presentation.

MAGIC JOHNSON

An example in the sports world of how the blessing phenomenon works in everyday life is Earvin "Magic" Johnson. Considered by many the best professional basketball player of all time, Magic was uniquely endowed: a 6'9" true point guard who could effectively play every position on the court. To this day, 6'9" point guards are unheard of.

In the sport of basketball, point guards are the primary ball handlers, the ones whose job it is to control the pace and flow of their team's offense. Traditionally, they tend to be among the shorter players on the team. Owing to this, Magic Johnson experienced resistance to the presentation of his unique gift at every level: high school, college and in the professional ranks. He was forced to defy naysayers, doubters and inhibitors constantly.

Magic had been the unique leader of championship teams in both high school and college. By the time he reached the professional ranks, he was *already* a champion. He was very familiar with champion leadership years before he became a

19-year-old rookie on what was largely a veteran Los Angeles Lakers basketball team. In his rookie season, Magic took the league by storm and led the Lakers to the first of five National Basketball Association (NBA) championships of his professional career. He would later go on to lead the "Dream Team" to an Olympic Gold Medal.

Magic Johnson was an expert ball handler and master of the *assist*, a pass from one player to another leading directly to a score. His unique combination of attributes enabled him to pioneer a fast-paced running style of basketball and in so doing helped to usher in a new exciting era in professional basketball. The basketball world had never seen anyone like him before, nor has it since. His primary focus on the court was bringing the best out in those around him. He did this by distributing the ball to his scoring teammates, rapidly and creatively. Shining in what he already was would cause everyone else on his team—indeed, the entire Lakers organization—to shine also. The more he shined, the more they shined. His greatness was in his unique ability to *spawn* greatness in others. Even as a rookie, his gloriously crafted identity was the catalyst for activating a higher level of greatness in older, more experienced teammates. Of all the great performance records attributed to Earvin "Magic" Johnson, the record that best exemplifies his greatness as a player doesn't even belong to him. It's the NBA's all-time *scoring* record held by his beloved teammate, Kareem Abdul-Jabbar. Magic Johnson rejuvenated his career in a way that no one else could have. The yet unsurpassed all-time scoring record of 38,387 is as much a testament to the greatness of Magic Johnson as it is to the steady endurance of the great Kareem Abdul-Jabbar.

Magic represented a cluster of puzzle-pieces around which a victorious picture was assembled, a picture known in the lore of NBA basketball as "Showtime."

Following his retirement from professional basketball, Magic continued to produce personal championships in his life. He continued to produce personal championships because he was *already* a champion with a unique proclivity for bringing the best out in others. He simply maintained and carried the same core champion identity into every arena of life he entered.

DAVID

In the days of old, when David was forced to flee the face of King Saul, he attracted a group of outcasts around him. The fact they were outcasts is what they had in common. David, however, was in possession of his personal blessing, his identity of victory. He shined with it in spite personal hardships and a long string of sad and unfortunate events. In time, David would become king, and that ragtag group of misfits who accompanied him would become the king's elite men-of-war, the core of the kingdom's royal forces.

Even though David's outcast status was indicative of defeat, his *experience* was victorious because he was victorious *already*—inwardly. In fact, he was victorious from the day he was anointed with the glory of his personal blessing by the prophet Samuel. David's glory *spawned* glory in those around him. Although he was experiencing a period of great loss and deprivation, that deprivation was only a phase in a victorious *experience*. He constituted that cluster of puzzle-pieces around whom a glorious picture would be assembled. There are countless other examples of this phenomenon in the long march of human history. You are one of them.

While operating in the blessing formula, it's also important to acknowledge the extent to which you benefit from what others bring to *your* life. The gravitational pull of your personal identity draws certain individuals into orbit around you, while others are repelled. Those who are drawn represent unique dimensions of your victorious experience. They actually fill the vital *spaces* of your life's glorious experience. You're one individual, but the various spaces of your life are filled when you shine in the glory of your personal blessing. Those who are blessed by the glow of your shine, in turn, enrich the quality of *your* experience. You're not in this life alone. You're a blessing to others and because of that, others are empowered to be a blessing to you. There will be multiple beneficiaries to your victorious experience, many of whom are not even on the stage of your life yet. They too will be a blessing to you.

DIVINE PERMISSION

Any man committed to doing anything extraordinary with his life tends to look for signs that signal the go-ahead, permission to proceed. You may look for confirmation in some situation, circumstance or environment. You may look to some event for a sign that the time is right. You may also look for confirmation in your various relationships. The trouble is that very little in the world around you is geared specifically toward reinforcing anything extraordinary from you. Even elements geared to benefit you to *some* extent can't be relied upon to affirm the validity of your identity of victory. Most people don't expect anything extraordinary from *themselves*; they certainly don't expect anything extraordinary from *you*. Most view any inclination towards things of an extraordinary nature ridiculous. The peculiar energy given off by aspirants to dreams of an extraordinary nature is considered strange, even foolhardy.

When you begin operating in your personal blessing, you'll be seen to be in rebellion against the social status quo, in rebellion against conventionality for the mere sake of rebellion. Those in your midst will view you as unduly optimistic or idealistic. Others may see you as being in over your head, foolishly wasting your time attempting the impossible. They'll quietly wait for your dreams and aspirations to be dashed. They'd prefer that you lived your life to the level of *their* expectations. They would have you to simply deal with life and living based on the way things appear; on how things seem; on how things look—outwardly. This is why it's important to understand that the permission you need to live wholeheartedly in your personal blessing doesn't come from anyone or anything outside of you. You need to look no further than the seed in your own possession for the signal to move forward victoriously with absolute confidence. Allow me to explain.

In light of the Law of Destiny, a seed actually *says* something to those in possession of it. Any seed, of whatever sort, makes an inaudible but unmistakable statement. The first thing it says is, "I have everything within me to produce the organism of my origin." Indeed, every cell and chromosome in perfect proportion necessary to reproduce the organism of a seed's origin is encapsulated within the seed itself. Nature has encapsulated the precise ingredients necessary for reproduction of the species.

The second thing a seed say is, "Not only do I represent the *substance* of the organism of my origin, I also represent *evidence* of that organism's existence." The fact the seed even exists is confirmation of the legitimacy of its source. The origin of any seed, for better or for worse, is an authentic entity, which can be reproduced.

The third thing a seed says is, "Don't let my relative small size cause you to underestimate my power. In spite of my tiny appearance, I'm very powerful." The fact is that a seed is miniscule in packaging, but mighty in potential. Because a seed has the ability to reproduce perpetually, its potential is unlimited. Even after the bearer of the seed has exited the scene, what he planted may continue to grow and reproduce forever.

The final and most important thing a seed says is, "By virtue of the fact that I'm in your possession, you have the ability; you have permission; indeed, you have the *right* to reproduce the organism of my origin. All you have to do is plant, feed and nurture me; the genetic blueprint within me will do the rest." The permission to be extraordinary comes by virtue of the fact that you're in possession of your extraordinary personal blessing: permission granted by possession. If you actually possess your personal blessing, you have divine permission to *be* extraordinary and for your life to produce accordingly.

R.E.S.T.

The greatest manifestations of history have three primary things in common. First, there was always a prior identity-change for those through whom the events occurred. Second, those through whom the events occurred developed an appreciation for their own uniqueness, *prior* to their achievement. Third, the great events or manifestations were largely unexpected by others; they were unanticipated.

You have now activated the most powerful elevating phenomenon ever introduced to man. But before you take another step, you need to be aware that what you *are* is nothing short of amazing. This is why you have the right to expect nothing less from your living experience.

We all appreciate positive reinforcement; we like it because it affirms our purpose. It makes us feel good about what we're doing with our lives. It inspires us to move forward in any given activity. As important as affirmative reinforcement is though, it's foolish to seek or expect it outside of you. Foreign reinforcement will always be inadequate when operating in your personal blessing. There can be no truly adequate outside reinforcement for the blessing phenomenon.

God "raiseth up the poor out of the dust, and lifteth up the beggar from the dunghill, to set them among princes, and to make them inherit the throne of glory . . ."[29] But even after the poor beggar receives his personal blessing, he still looks dusty and smells of dung. This is all that others can possibly perceive. Although he's blessed, he simply doesn't look nor does he smell like a king who has inherited a throne. As such, others aren't going to treat him as royalty.

Similarly, others cannot adequately reinforce you. They can't view you through the lens of your personal blessing. They can't view you the way the Almighty views you or the way you now view yourself. Others can't help undervaluing you. This is true even in the case of those who are supportive of you. They want the best *for* you, but can't see the best *in* you. It's not that they're insensitive to you or that they don't love you. But their expectations of you are simply too low. They expect *something* from you, but nothing amazing, nothing extraordinary and nothing monumental. You're heading far above what others expect of you. Others can't possibly provide you with appropriate fuel. The fuel they can provide doesn't burn *nearly* hot enough for what you are. At best, they can provide you with low-level reinforcement, the equivalent to pumping regular gasoline into a high-powered rocket—wholly inadequate. Rocket fuel is required. Anything less is insufficient. The only person who can provide you with rocket fuel is *you*.

Everything functional requires some sort of fuel. The fuel is specific to the organism in question. Animals of different types require various kinds of food. Sometimes the food a

---

[29]   I SAMUEL 2:8

particular species requires for survival seems strange. Vultures, for example, thrive by eating rotting flesh. Humans require certain foods for healthy survival. The variety is wide-ranging and humans the world over flourish from eating any number of different types of food. Organisms big and small die from lack of proper nourishment.

Your personal blessing is a living organism requiring a specific type of food in order to thrive. There is nothing more powerful than a well-fed, well-nourished personal blessing. Possessing a personal blessing is much like having a child; quite a responsibility. If you don't provide it with food, it won't eat. Food deprivation ends in starvation and eventually death. Embracing your personal blessing is a life-altering event, so your commitment to caring for it is vital.

In order to thrive in the glorious majesty of your personal blessing, you must provide it with Repetitive Elevating Self-Talk. The greater the distance between your personal blessing and your point of departure, the more repetitive elevating self-talk is required. This is how you must reinforce yourself. You are amazing; this is true, but no one knows this better than you do. So, if *you* don't acknowledge it, no one else will; they simply can't. Don't be afraid to declare your self-truth *to* yourself. You are what you are, and what your life is now producing is amazing, wonderful and monumental. You know full well what manner of seed you planted into the soil of your mind. You're certain of the seed's origin. You know exactly where it came from; more specifically, you know exactly *when* it came from. You must not be afraid to acknowledge your own greatness to yourself. It's through what you repetitively *say* to yourself that empowers you to operate in the corresponding capacity. Of all the words spoken to or about you, the words you speak to yourself *about* yourself matter most. Repetitive elevating self-talk is the fuel required for your personal blessing.

Affirmative words spoken about you, to you, by you, are personal blessing food. Negating words spoken about you, to you, by you, are personal blessing poison. If you're not willing to feed your personal blessing what it requires to thrive in your life, it is better that you don't embrace it at all. Leave it where you found it. The tragedy of allowing your personal blessing to starve is worse than not having discovered it in the first place.

How does one engage in repetitive elevating self-talk? The process calls for you to do exactly what it sounds like: repetitively declare your personal blessing to yourself. Your own tongue is the public address system of your mind. Your mind will always stop to listen to your tongue. It takes heed to the words formed and spoken by your tongue. The identity dimension of your mind is the control center of your life, so it is imperative that your tongue be under your conscious control. You must seize full control of your tongue, and make it say what you need it to say, as it relates to the identity dimension of your mind.

"So then faith cometh by hearing, and hearing by the word of God."[30] Your personal blessing is the word of God for your life. If Abram had not heard "the word of God"—*Abraham*—for his personal life he wouldn't have been able to produce according to his vision, because he wouldn't have been able to embrace *Abraham* as his personal identity. The key is that he received it

---

[30] ROMANS 10:17

and then *repeated* it to himself. Likewise, after you receive "the word of God" for your life, the more you *repeat* it, the more you'll *hear* it, and the more you'll be able to operate according to that word, causing your life to produce accordingly.

Powerful information is revealed to you through your personal blessing. Your answers to the Blessing Question reveal what the Almighty has called you to be right here, right now, in this very moment. In essence, He has declared, "You are_____." Now you need to call *yourself* what He has called you. You must engage in this practice constantly! You must reinforce yourself by repetitively declaring to yourself, "You are . . . You are . . . You are . . . ," filling in the blank according to the *ultimate* version of you.

You may choose to declare repetitively any aspect of your personal blessing, depending on what aspect needs to be fed at any given time. It's all you; it's all yours. You have a right to it all, in part or in whole, at all times. However you choose to engage repetitive elevating self-talk, in whatever order you choose to do it, declare your personal blessing to yourself as much and as often as you possibly can. Set aside time to feed your personal blessing by vocalizing it. Build it up through speaking it to yourself. This is an important aspect of activating personal ultimacy. Employ the use soft earplugs, which will enable you to hear yourself whispering or speaking softly.

Fasting while performing repetitive elevating self-talk is extremely effective in internalizing your personal blessing. Owing to food deprivation, your ability to doubt and to resist is inhibited. You simply won't have the energy to doubt or resist what you're taking in. So that when the fasting is over, you'll discover that the thing you were meditating upon during the fast has become a prominent aspect of your moment-to-moment reality. In a short period of time, you will declare to yourself, with easy and confident resolve, "I am_____, and all else is relative!" Despite all contradictory stimuli, you will *be* the ultimate version of you. You will rise to the occasion. The ultimate version of you will be normal for you. You'll look yourself in the mirror and realize that you really are exactly what your personal blessing says you are, right here, right now, in this very moment. And your life is producing accordingly.

"Death and life are in the power of the tongue,"[31] but if you relinquish your authority, you will be subject to all sorts of arbitrary elements. You'll accept, meditate upon and repeat what other elements and factors are saying about you. Through default, you'll be a slave to something, somewhere or someone. Your situation is constantly saying something about you. Your circumstance is constantly saying something about you. Your environment is constantly saying something about you. Events are constantly saying something about you. Others are constantly saying something about you, verbally or non-verbally, through their attitudes or dispositions toward you. This is why you must constantly say something to *yourself* about you, lest you unconsciously abdicate your throne and begin internalizing that which is projected onto or around you. Your own tongue has a job to perform as it relates to you being one with your personal blessing. This is why you must seize full control of this function and utilize it accordingly.

---

[31] PROVERBS 18:21

A strong, well-fed identity of victory can move mountains and subdue kingdoms. Through repetitive elevating self-talk, a keen sense of self will lift you to unprecedented levels in your own consciousness, and self-doubt will be eliminated from your personal living experience. You *are* exactly what your personal blessing says you are, right here, right now, in this very moment. Feed this reality. Build up this reality and accept it for what it is!

THE BASIS OF YOUR CONFIDENCE

Man is at his best when operating in absolute confidence. The only question Yashua (Jesus) asked Peter when he rescued him from sinking, immediately after Peter walked on top of the water, was, "[W]herefore didst thou doubt?"[32] In other words, "Why did you doubt yourself?" Doubt will turn you into a *self*-saboteur. You will sabotage yourself through doubt. The greatest, most stunning events, developments and human spectacles of history emerged from individuals and groups operating in absolute confidence. The Almighty *requires* confidence in the blessed man. "Cast not away therefore your confidence, which hath great recompence of reward."[33] Build up your confidence by keeping your personal blessing well fed. Confidence is the human enhancer. Whatever you do confidently will be *enhanced* tremendously. Confidence causes everything you are and do to be more effective. Confidence makes you

---

[32]   MATTHEW 14:31
[33]   HEBREWS 10:35

shine. It makes you glow. Your confidence will express the worthiness of your vision, the worthiness of your life's mission. What the Almighty has placed within you is worth manifesting; it's worth living for. Your confidence is an indispensable tool in its manifestation.

Confidence must be self-generated; it must come from within. Your confidence is tied inextricably to a well-fed personal blessing. Your confidence stabilizes you. It prevents you from being tossed about mentally and emotionally. It keeps you focused on what you *are* and the role you play. It helps you to keep the end in proper perspective during the phases and changes associated with the process of *being*. Your victory is energized by your confidence.

The basis of your confidence is very important. The foundation upon which your confidence rests must never be associated with any manner of situations, circumstances, environments, events or other people. These aren't safe foundations upon which to base your confidence. If any of these elements constitutes the basis of your confidence, you'll be *subject* to these elements; they'll *own* you. A man is subject to that upon which he places his confidence. Your confidence will be shattered when based on arbitrary, unreliable, changeable elements. Individuals are broken, mere shells of what they could've and should've been because they based their confidence upon unreliable factors. Situations change; circumstances change; environments change; events change; people change.

Base your confidence on the immutability of the Law of Destiny. **Identity Produces Destiny!** What a thing *is* determines what it can and will produce. It will never be otherwise. This principle will never be abrogated, never violated. The Almighty's eternal seed principle is peerless and full proof. It has never failed and it never will.

The world has never experienced one like you. You are extraordinary. You are magnificent and what you're doing *because* of what you are is amazing. Feed your personal blessing what it requires. Reinforce yourself! You're the most interesting person you know. Be what you are with absolute confidence, with the full force of what your victorious identity portends. The Law of Destiny and the Law of Human Nature are eternal, and can be relied upon eternally. Rest your confidence upon this reality. Move wholeheartedly into the glory of your destiny by continuing to shine in your glorious identity, with absolute confidence.

5

EXTREME CONTRADICTIONS

"The man must be so much that he must make all circumstances indifferent—put all means into the shade. This all great men are and do."

—Ralph Waldo Emerson

CONTRADICTION DOMINATION

There are extreme contradictions between your personal blessing and everything else going on around you. Nothing in the world outside of you bears witness to what your personal blessing has revealed about you. The blessing of Abraham is in effect a one-witness phenomenon. You're the only one who can bear witness to the validity of your personal blessing. The dream, the vision from which your personal blessing was extracted, is yours personally. But your situation doesn't bear witness to it; your circumstance doesn't bear witness to it; your environment doesn't bear witness to it; no outside events bear witness to it, and others don't bear witness to it.

One-witness personal blessings are the most powerful in the world because when they bloom, they're stunning; they catch everyone by surprise. Personal identities that contradict all else around them are the bases of the most extraordinary manifestations of the human experience. If the contradictions of your life were slight or subtle, they wouldn't pose such a daunting challenge to you. But the contradictions revealed by your personal blessing are stark, blatant and obvious; so much so, that if you didn't understand the process, they could actually make you feel ridiculous. Realize that there would be no contradictions if you weren't so wonderfully blessed. Without your personal blessing, you'd fit right into the madness going on around you. In the absence of your personal blessing, you'd blend right in. Instead of representing a *contradiction*, you'd represent a *product*. You'd be a product of your situation; a product of your circumstance; a product of your environment;

a product of events and a product of the whims of others. You'd be losing miserably, but there would be no contradiction.

Your personal blessing is the *ultimate* version of you. What you fit into isn't even visible to the naked eye. You only fit into the vision that you have for your life. You only fit into what your life is producing as a result of embracing your personal blessing.

The natural inclination of humans is to fit in some place. No one wants to be a misfit. Instinctively, we want to eliminate contradictions from our lives. We're conditioned from an early age to reconcile contradictions. As small children, we had toy shapes designed to fit into corresponding holes. The square didn't fit into the circle; the triangle didn't fit into the star, and so on. We want things to fit; we want things to match. We want fitting relationships. We want the actions of the people in our lives to match their words. We want the performance of the actors to match the scene for which the stage has been set. If for any reason things don't fit, we make changes and adjustments in order to reconcile the differences. In short, we want the things of life to correspond.

The test of the blessed, however, isn't to *eliminate* contradictions. The test of the blessed isn't to *reconcile* contradictions. The test of the blessed is the ability to *dominate* contradictions, by sheer force of character. If you don't dominate contradictions, then contradictions are going to dominate *you*; and if any sort of domination is to occur, you need to be the *dominator* and not the dominated. You must play out the snow scene confidently against the backdrop of a stage set for the desert. You must confidently live out one scenario against the contradictory backdrop of another. This is what the blessing of Abraham demanded from the very beginning. The fact is you are more real than your situation is; you are more legitimate than your circumstance is; you are more authentic than your environment is; you are more powerful than the events around you are; and you are more credible than those who are opposed to you are.

Situations, circumstances, environments and events are largely products of the consciousness of man. They are arbitrary human projections, subject to change from one moment to the next. Product can never be superior to source. As such, you must never be intimidated by what others have produced or are projecting upon the earth. Never be intimidated by the propaganda of others, whether cognitive or material, present or past. You are no less authentic than anyone else is, and their projections are only human phenomena. You must dance to your own tune and stride to your own rhythm, though the loudspeakers of the world are trumpeting something completely different. Your life will always produce according to what you are—*inwardly*.

Contradictions actually work *for* the blessed man. Contradictions reveal your uniqueness. They reveal how extraordinary you really are. No contradiction; no elevation. As a kite relies on wind pulling *against* it, your personal blessing relies on contradictions. As a star relies on darkness, your personal blessing relies on contradictions. Contradictions expose the distinctions between you and every*one* else. They expose the distinctions between you and every*thing* else.

Contradictions reveal your glory, the supernatural glow of your personal blessing.

"[W]alk worthy of the vocation wherewith ye are called."[34] You are worthy of the blessing you've been given. Defy everyone and everything suggesting that you are *unworthy* of your personal blessing. Dominate contradictions by remaining true to your personal blessing at all times. You have a God-given right to live in the glory of your own personal blessing, the ultimate version of *you*. Your life must declare, "I am!" in the midst of all that says, "You are not!" Know this; if you were unworthy of your personal blessing, you never would have come into possession of it. The only reason you *have* it is because you were worthy *of* it.

Endurance is the key. The price you pay for the manifestation of your vision is endurance. Endurance and patience constitute the coin of the blessing realm. The sacred formula doesn't allow for discounts. You must pay in full. Your personal blessing is a lifelong commitment. The tree is what it is long before we see its fruit. Your endurance will reveal the glorious impression of the ultimate version of you and all that it entails. Don't compromise the integrity of your personal blessing. If you'll live in your victory, your victory will live in you and color all that you do. This is the way of the blessed.

---

[34] EPHESIANS 4:1

THE CENTRALITY OF IDENTITY

All life revolves around the element of identity. Even the Almighty, the Supreme Being, identifies Himself by declaring, "I AM."[35] The Most High is the Supreme Identity.

Natural identities are vital to the human experience. They are important aspects of belonging. This is why we celebrate them. At birth, we celebrate the new baby. We want to know his name, how much he weighs, whom he favors and such. We celebrate the new parents and grandparents. We acknowledge the new brother or sister, the new aunt or uncle, the new cousin, the new niece or nephew. When the child goes off to school, we acknowledge the fact that he's now a student. When he completes school, we acknowledge the fact that he is now a graduate. When he gets married, we celebrate that he's now a husband and the day he becomes a father himself, the cycle of natural identities continues.

Throughout life, there are continual identity augmentations. The reason we take note of them is we know intuitively that identity is what gives force, shape and perspective to life. We have annual celebrations of natural identities. Birthday celebrations acknowledge the anniversary of one's birth. Marriage anniversaries commemorate the day one became a spouse. In some parts of the world, Mother's Day is set aside to acknowledge the identity of mother and all that accompanies that wonderful identity. Similarly, Father's Day is celebrated. Family reunions acknowledge and celebrate the continuity of

---

[35] EXODUS 3:14

a family's identity. Natural identities are vital to the human experience.

Personal identity, however, differs from natural identity. Personal identity is what distinguishes you as a unique individual, *inwardly*. Personal identity transcends all other identities. It outranks and commands all others. It governs all others. Personal identity determines what *manner* of man you are and what *manner* of whatever else you are.

"When thou wast little in thine own sight, wast thou not made the head . . . ?"[36] Your personal blessing is a mind-expanding, elevating experience. Your self-concept has been dramatically recast. Your personal blessing forces you to confront yourself on a completely new level. All of a sudden, you have to accept something about yourself for which you have no prior experience, for which nothing bears witness. You have no family background or visible qualifications for what your personal blessing has revealed about you. You are now forced to confront your experience and the lack thereof. This self-confrontation is born of the fact that you've never viewed or thought of yourself so grandly before. For the first time, you've discovered that you had been grossly under-representing yourself. You had been living far beneath your personal privilege as an individual. You had been operating in a degraded version of yourself. You have now stepped into a version of you that you never knew. This is uncharted territory for you. Your personal blessing is a radical departure from what you had come to accept about yourself and your life.

---

[36]   I SAMUEL 15:17

Just as you acknowledge dimension-adding identities that are natural and common to the human experience, you must be willing to acknowledge your personal blessing, the *ultimate* version of you, which is your most significant identity. The spirit of your personal blessing permeates every other area of your life; it rules every other aspect of your life. Like a marriage, you should celebrate it as a lifelong commitment. You ought to mark this time, this period, this phase of your life. For the first time, you've entered the realm of the highest possible living experience available to you, the highest possible level of freedom and liberation available to you. This is as close to heaven on earth as you or anyone else can get. Life will only get better for you. Prepare yourself; you've now entered the monumental phase of your life. You're now living in the version of you intended by the Most High from the beginning.

A HIGHER UNDERSTANDING

You have experienced a personal awakening. You now realize that you're more wonderful, more significant, more magnificent, more special and more gifted than you ever knew. You have now passed through a divine threshold, a divine matrix. You must get over the shock of your own unique greatness and come to terms with it. These are your moments. This is your new normal. Though you may not have realized it, you are uniquely qualified to handle all that accompanies your personal blessing. The qualifications are *within* the identity itself. The more you remain true to your personal blessing, the more you'll witness its activity in your life. You possess dormant faculties of which you are unaware, faculties that are activated only when you fully embrace your personal blessing. This is why you must not shrink from living wholeheartedly in your greatness. Unknown powers and forces will be revealed from within you; but you *must* remain true.

The gap between your new personal identity and the old is huge. A complete embrace of your personal blessing is the only thing that successfully bridges the gap. The consciousness-gap between your personal blessing and your previous self-concept reveals a stark contrast, a contrast that can be embarrassing. This contrast exposes just how lowly you actually viewed yourself. It's important to note that your lowly state was not altogether your fault. You were vulnerable to degradation because you lacked understanding. You lacked specific knowledge. You were a victim to degradation because of what you didn't know. But a full embrace of your personal blessing will reconcile and repair the breach.

The Almighty has been guiding you toward and preparing you for this glorious dimension your entire life. Your possession of your personal blessing is not an accident. The fact that you are now holding this book in your hands is by divine design. Now is not the time for intimidation and fear; you've come too far for that; you've been through too much for that. Now's the time to receive the full glory your life has to offer. You're entitled to the treasure you have found within your noble vision. You must step into it triumphantly and accept it for all that it is.

The beautiful but harsh reality about the blessing phenomenon is that it doesn't coddle you. The ultimate truth about you to which you've been exposed is something you simply have to accept. You must adjust and raise your mind to its level. You have to get used to it and cooperate with it. The Almighty doesn't lower His standard of you to where you are. You must ascend to *His* high calling. You must rise; you must be one with your personal blessing. The blessing of Abraham is uncompromising; it's fixed and firm. It has to be this way because your personal blessing establishes a new standard of you—*for* you. It's the standard against which you must gauge, measure and estimate yourself and all else. Everything and everyone is *relative* to your personal blessing. The ultimate version of you is your life's major reference point. You must engage life from this vantage point. Your personal blessing empowers you to view your life as you actually *should* be viewing it—from the top.

Your personal blessing is the hub to which all the elements of your world are connected. Every aspect of your life now hangs on the linchpin of your personal blessing. It's the axis about which all else spins. It's the keystone upholding the archway leading to your destiny. Your personal blessing is your manhood—your wholeness. It's not a matter of how others define you; it's only a matter of how you define yourself. In the grand milieu of public opinion, it's never a matter of what others think of *you*, but always a matter of what you think of *them*. Don't take your personal blessing lightly. Don't play yourself falsely; the stakes are very high.

It took Abram 99 years to be exposed to the ultimate version of himself. It shouldn't take anyone else that long to come to terms with his own treasure. The Almighty used Abram's long illustrious life to reveal the blessing formula and the two eternal principles upon which it rests. These elements have been revealed once and for all. They are profound but simple and easy to understand. Every man should be in possession of his own personal blessing, which reveals the *ultimate* version of him—*to* him. The upshot of Abram's story was that he was too small in his own sight. As great, wise and able as Abram was, *Abraham* was greater, wiser and abler. The life of Abraham could produce what the life of Abram couldn't. Such is the case for your life. Allow the *ultimate* version of you to produce what the *previous* versions of you could *not* produce.

Although Abram was very rich already, he wasn't experiencing personal ultimacy. He wasn't operating in the greatest version of himself. He wasn't fulfilled. Abram had a dream that money could not buy. The identity of Abram wasn't good enough to manifest the loftiness to which he aspired. The personal identity of Abram didn't present *any* faith-contradictions. He was *born* into that identity. Vis-à-vis *Abraham*, Abram was a typical, natural, non-contradictory personal identity. This is why Abram was limited to producing typical, natural, non-contradictory things. Nothing in Abram's life bore witness to him being *father of many nations*. Instead, he was subject to daunting contradictory circumstances—old age and a barren wife, with whom he shared a dream.

Abraham, however, was the *ultimate* version of Abram. As such, Abraham produced extraordinary things; he produced in the realm of the supernatural. Abram believed the Almighty's "promise of the Spirit through faith."[37] He believed that if he

---

[37]   GALATIANS 3:14

would simply embrace the identity of victory extracted from his vision of victory, *in the present*, with absolute confidence, his life would produce accordingly; and it did just that, vindicating his faithful lifelong experience. Abram embraced *Abraham* as his personal identity. Abram was not intimidated by contradictory circumstances. Through a full embrace of his identity of victory, he dominated the contradictions that once dominated him. Isaac, the son of promise, was the triumphant *fruit* of the seed that was *Abraham*.

SELF-MASTERY

Abram was exposed to the blessing formula, to the Law of Destiny and the Law of Human Nature. He mastered these principles by embracing *Abraham* as his personal identity, *in the present*, with absolute confidence. He was able to dominate extreme contradictions because, for the first time, he understood the *source* of destiny. There was no longer any reason for him to be frustrated by contradictory circumstances. He understood for the first time that personal destiny is determined by personal identity, not by situations or circumstances. He now understood that he had the ability and the right to control the outcome and quality of his own living experience on a monumental scale. Abraham bequeathed this sacred wisdom to the inhabitants of the earth, a beautiful inheritance indeed. It's the *height* of human understanding, the *height* of divine wisdom.

Abraham is a blessing to *all* the families of the earth, by way of the wisdom introduced to humanity through his life. Your challenge is to embrace fully the ultimate version of *you*. Your answers to the Blessing Question expose extreme contradictions and contrasts, but you must not be afraid to experience yourself fully on a higher plane. You must allow your personal blessing to permeate your mind and your thinking. This is the only way you'll be able to *dominate* extreme contradictions and contrasts. Your personal blessing *is* your reality.

Mind-control is necessary; it's vital. Control your own mind. Do this by controlling the identity dimension of your mind. Brainwashing is a good thing, as long as *you* are the one with the soap and water. Don't let anyone else brainwash you in the realm of personal identity. That domain is yours—*alone*. You must be in full control of your self-concept at all times. If you don't claim the ultimate version of your own manhood, other influences will. If you don't respect the ultimate version of you, you'll be fuel for the fires of others and not even realize it. You'll suddenly find yourself cast in someone else's scenario; a mere prop in someone else's degrading play, a pawn in the losing chess game of your own life. You'll be used for someone else's nefarious purposes. It's your responsibility to maintain your personal blessing, come what may. Your self-concept must not and cannot be dependent on any outside reinforcement. Remember, nothing outside of you adequately reinforces you. There's nothing but shifting contradictory propaganda all around you. Don't be dismayed by it. Just be true to the ultimate version of you at all times.

INHERITED CONSTRICTION

It is possible to be born into the victory of others as well as it is to be born into the defeat of others. Sometimes, being born into the victory of others isn't appreciably different from being born into the defeat of others. In light of what you've learned of the blessing formula, you may already realize how both scenarios can be equally constricting.

There are families who are immensely successful in business, sports, medicine, education or any number of other human endeavors. Those born into such families weren't around when the foundations of their families' successes were laid. They didn't fight any of the battles that enabled their families to be positioned the way they are. They simply inherited what others left behind. They picked up where previous generations left off. They perpetuated already-established legacies. They could of course make adjustments when necessary, but the successful courses were already established, the primary roads already paved.

There are peoples born into victorious nations and cultures the world over. But these individuals weren't the original revolutionaries. They weren't the ones who established the national principles for which they'll live and die today. They weren't the ones who decided to put their collective nationalist foot down and stand for what they believed. They simply inherited the values, the principles and the ways of life brought forth and left behind by others. These seemingly fortunate inheritors didn't actually *earn* their elevated place in the world. Others bequeathed it to them.

When you're born into a victorious national or cultural identity, you inherit the corresponding national or cultural state of mind. Indeed, you inherit the entire national or cultural destiny structure. This dynamic is often played out in history. Current generations pursue a national or cultural agenda set in motion by previous generations, now long gone. In much the same way, children born into "royal families" inherit a sense of importance, whether real or imagined. They inherit a sense of royal responsibility, even though the progenitor of the "royal" line is long gone.

Being born into someone else's victory *can*, however, be limiting and stifling. The heavy burden of perpetuating a restrictive legacy can all but smother the extraordinary uniqueness and originality of the inheritor. Inheriting the victory of others doesn't exempt a man from the extreme contradictions exposed by his personal blessing. In fact, the contradictions may even be starker. The blessing of Abraham isn't bound to reconcile any legacy you may have inherited. It's unlimited and unrestricted by any legacy into which you may have been born. It's quite possible—indeed *likely*—that the ultimate version of you far exceeds any victory you've inherited from others. Many times what seems to be an advantage is really a disadvantage.

Think of an acorn that inherits a golden flowerpot. Even though the flowerpot may be ornate and beautiful, what the acorn *contains* is greater than what its inheritance will allow it to realize. It's not that the flowerpot is unable to provide a beautiful nurturing environment for a time; it can. But a foolish loyalty to its inheritance will turn what the acorn contains into a caricature. It'll forever be a bonsai oak, a miniature oak. Instead of the glory of the pasture, it will forever only be a plant. The context of its presentation will be glorious and exquisite, but at the expense of the substance it contains. The potted oak will be a mutation, shamefully overshadowed by weeds, shrubs and bushes.

It's also possible to be born into someone else's defeat. There are individuals who have been born into severe dysfunction, ranging from acute to chronic. Many are born into families torn apart by previous events. Many a family has had previous experiences causing the majority of its current-generation members to be *self*-destructive. Persons born into such families inherit the effects of previous experiences, traumatic events of which they are largely unaware. Individuals born into such families are not the ones who suffered the defeats; they simply inherited the losses of those who did. Individuals born into defeated, dysfunctional families are simply the inheritors of the debilitating values, principles and ways of life left behind by others.

Peoples the world over are born into nations and cultures that have been defeated, subdued and subjugated by others. Persons born into such scenarios are *indirectly* defeated. They weren't there when the battles were fought. Their defeat is vicarious. They *inherited* defeat. They were born *into* someone else's deficiencies. They were born relegated to the low rung of the social scale. To them, bottom dwelling is their natural place in society; it's all they know. Bottom dwelling is normal for them. They were born subject to the vicious dehumanizing stereotypes and stigmas propagated by others, and they internalize that which is projected. Essentially, these individuals are born defeated. They didn't even get the chance to fight their own fight. The entire society in which they live reinforces their degraded status. Their lowly status is woven into the psychosocial fabric, baked into the cake of the society itself, and the subtle nuances of the social milieu bear constant witness. Their lowly position doesn't need to be verbalized; it's already understood.

Nothing extraordinary or monumental is expected of those born into defeated nations or cultures. Not surprisingly, these individuals don't expect anything extraordinary or monumental of themselves. The same standards used to gauge and measure the achievements of others are not applied to persons born into defeated nations or cultures. Their success is gauged and measured using a different scale. What they do isn't even considered to be in the same category as what others do. They're perceived as the dregs of society and are classified as such in the minds of all, including themselves.

The destiny structure of those born into defeat bears witness to a collective identity born out of an experience of which they weren't even a party. Their destiny structure was prescribed before they arrived. Any deviation from the norm places them out of bounds in the minds of others, particularly those closest to them. Deviation makes them strange, peculiar and even radical in the minds of others. Deviation from what's expected exposes them to extreme social and institutional contradictions. There is tremendous pressure for them to maintain status quo.

Perhaps the most tragic thing about those born into someone else's defeat—whether a family, nation or culture—is that in many cases they don't even realize it; and when they do, they can't tell exactly what was lost. They don't know because they weren't among those who lost it. Even if they did want to fight, they're unaware of that for which they should be fighting. They can't fight effectively because they don't know why they are fighting. They can't fight effectively if they don't even have an appreciation for what's at stake.

KING JOSIAH

Long ago, there was a boy-king whose name was Josiah. He was born into someone else's defeat. Prior to his birth, the royal family had descended into severe dysfunction. The kingdom was in shambles. Josiah's grandfather, who had been king 55 years, was wicked. His father's short reign followed in those footsteps. Josiah's father died young, murdered by his own servants. At the tender age of eight, Josiah inherited the throne of a kingdom that was a shell of what it was ordained to be. He hadn't been exposed to the greatness of the kingdom. He hadn't witnessed the kingdom's glorious history. But as he matured, Josiah had one significant thing going for him. He had a *vision* of victory. He had a dream, a goal, and an ambition. He had a mind to do something wonderful with the kingdom he inherited. He ordered the deteriorating temple repaired and beautified.

The temple, as it turns out, was the historical nucleus of the kingdom, the centerpiece of the realm. As king, he figured wisely, the temple was the appropriate place to spawn any renaissance. The work began. While the temple underwent renovation, the high priest himself found the ancient book of the covenant. It had fallen out of use over the many years of degradation and had been stored away within the inner chambers of the temple. This document was very important. The lawgiver, the great prophet Moses, handed down the book of the covenant many generations prior. The book of the covenant was the kingdom's Constitution. The book of the covenant was the basis upon which Samuel the prophet would later established the kingdom, and it's the thing to which King David was beholden during his illustrious reign. The book of the covenant contained what *manner* of kingdom theirs was supposed to be.

The kingdom had drifted far from the course for which it was ordained. When the book was brought to King Josiah, he read it. Immediately, he began to grieve the lowly and tragic state to which the kingdom had fallen. The book of the covenant gave King Josiah reason to mourn. For the first time he had a basis of comparison; he had a standard against which to measure what he was witnessing. For the first time he could see the gulf between where his kingdom was and where it was supposed to be. He took *instant* action to restore his society to the glorious position for which it was instituted. He was able to act forcefully and deliberately because, among other things, he learned what manner of king he was supposed to be. There was now a standard against which to measure himself. The book of the covenant contained the provision for Josiah's hereditary royal identity. He discovered that the kingdom he inherited was actually Yahweh's (God's) kingdom. He discovered the throne he inherited was actually King David's throne. He came to understand that, as a direct descendant of King David, he was the latest installment of what is an everlasting royal seed. His job was to represent honorably the house of David—the royal lineage. His royal responsibility was to acknowledge, proclaim and execute divine law and authority throughout the kingdom.

King Josiah developed a powerful sense of self. He began operating according to a new destiny structure and the kingdom experienced a great revival because of his awakening. The royal citizens of the kingdom experienced a great restoration unlike any witnessed previously.

Notice the divine symbolism of the blessing phenomenon at work in the story of King Josiah. The seed that enabled him to manifest greatness was contained within his personal vision—his personal ambition. Within the temple itself, which was the focal point of Josiah's vision of victory, was the seed that had the power to reproduce the fruit from whence it came. The original fruit was a godly dominion of righteousness. The temple was the core of this dominion. In the core was the only seed that could regenerate the glory of the dominion. The seed, in this case, was the book of the covenant, which contained the well-established identities of every function and position of the kingdom, including that of the king himself. The book of the covenant contained the DNA, the specific genetic blueprint, of a great and glorious institution. Josiah planted that seed and witnessed a glory unseen in generations.

To be sure, Josiah's blessing revealed extreme contradictions, but he *dominated* those contradictions by operating in absolute confidence. By dominating the extreme contradictions posed by his family's previous dysfunction, Josiah was able to revive the kingdom. He wasn't intimidated by social decay, low expectations or wicked lifestyles of previous royals.

IDENTITY INVINCIBILITY

The Almighty has established a divine liberating provision for the human family. This provision is for those born into full-functioning but stifling victory and also for those born into horrific, inhibiting defeat. This divine liberating provision is for those born into advantage and for those born into disadvantage. It's for those who find themselves in situations, circumstances and environments of all sorts. The sacred formula empowers individuals to win their own fights, regardless of all forces stacked against them. This ancient formula reveals things about individuals they never knew about themselves. It awakens individuals to a dimension of life that defies what their natural senses reveal to them. Like King Josiah's discovery, your answers to the Blessing Question contain sacred knowledge, sacred information that you must take seriously.

You must never allow yourself to be dominated by the extreme contradictions that are revealed by your personal blessing. Your identity of victory must be *invincible*. Identity invincibility is vital to a blossoming personal blessing. Your identity of victory must be indomitable, unshakeable and unbreakable. This is your fight and you must not lose it. You simply can't afford to lose this fight. You must prevail triumphantly. There is too much at stake and you now know what the stakes are. You are what your personal blessing says you are; all else is relative!

The psychological and social constrictions left behind by previous generations were constrictions to your personal identity. The sacred formula gives you the ability to thrive, regardless of the extent to which you were previously limited. Critical to thriving freely is the need to be absolutely true to the *ultimate* version of you. When you answered the Blessing Question, what sacred information did you discover about yourself? Are you keeping those sacred truths at the forefront of your mind at all times? Are you living fully according to those truths, regardless of all else? Are you locked in to the *ultimate* version of you? Are you *one* with the highest version of you, the most wonderful version of you, right here, right now, in this very moment? Are you _____*right now*? Because in order to receive the highest possible living experience available to you—freedom and liberation at the *highest* possible level—you must *fully* accept and acknowledge the *ultimate* truth about you, and stand to it come what may.

"And ye shall know the truth, and the truth shall make you free."[38] The *seed* will be true to itself, but you must be true to the seed. There is no reason for your life to be constricted or limited. Your personal blessing has provided you with specific knowledge of deep and profound personal truth. Knowledge of this type can only usher in freedom at the highest level. Fully understanding and embracing your personal blessing gives you the advantage necessary to dominate extreme contradictions in whatever forms they may present themselves. Your personal blessing must be invincible.

---

[38] JOHN 8:32

THE POWER OF PERSPECTIVE

The one thing any identity guarantees is a corresponding perspective. When I speak of perspective, I'm not speaking of what you see, but of how you see it. I'm speaking of the vantage point from which you view life. The state of mind that comes from a particular identity will cause you to lock into a particular perspective. Generally speaking, we're all looking at the same things in life, but we don't perceive the same things, because we're not viewing things from the same point of view.

All perspectives are legitimate, in that they're true manifestations of some identity. It's your personal perspective that provides the launching point for the bulk of your identity structure. Your perspective is by far the most prominent aspect of your destiny structure. If your destiny structure were a tree, your perspective constitutes the trunk. Your agenda, attitude, aura, words and actions constitute the leaves and branches; the outcome and quality of your living experience constitute the fruit.

The *source* of your entire destiny structure is of course your personal identity, but the interactions of life are strictly within the purview of your *perspective*. It's your perspective that shapes your agenda. Your personal priorities stem from your perspective. It's your perspective that crystallizes your purpose, responsibilities and personal duties. Your perspective is a motivating factor. It's a guiding force. Your attitude about people, places and things stems from your perspective. Your disposition regarding what constitutes right and wrong, appropriate and inappropriate stems from your perspective.

It's your perspective that governs your aura. The gravitational force generated by your life emanates from your perspective. Individuals are drawn to or repelled from you because of your personal polarity, which is governed by your perspective. Your perspective channels your polarity, the invisible force of push and pull surrounding your life.

Perspective governs both speech and silence. Your perspective determines your words and the tone with which you use those words. The depth and seriousness of your words stem from your perspective. Your behavior pattern stems from your perspective. Your strategy stems from your perspective. The parameters and guidelines within which you live stem from your perspective. Your body language stems from your perspective. The way you move and all your mannerisms stem from your perspective.

Understand, though, that as prominent a role as your perspective plays in your living experience, it is *not* the source of your destiny. *Identity* is the source. Perspective, as powerful and decisive a role as it plays in your life, in the final analysis, is a mere *outgrowth* of identity. Accordingly, there are strong, dominant perspectives, and there are weak, submissive perspectives, depending on the *manner* of identity from which it stems.

Embracing your personal blessing provides you with a strong, dominant perspective. A strong, dominant perspective enables you to frame the experience of your own life. It empowers you to project the circumference of your own life's reality. A strong, dominant perspective bears witness to the divine dominion the Almighty has given man upon the earth. It gives you a clear-cut agenda. It gives you the appropriate attitude for your life, an aura that powerfully attracts and repels. It gives you meaningful, effective words. A strong, dominant perspective gives you bold and decisive action.

It is better to be weak from a perspective of strength than to be strong from a perspective of weakness, because in time, your perspective—not what you see but *how* you see it—will turn your weakness into a strength or your strength into a weakness. When your perspective is weak, it doesn't matter how strong you are. The only thing you'll perceive is the strength of the opposition. As such, you'll be disadvantaged. Likewise, when your perspective is strong, it doesn't matter how weak you are. The only thing you'll perceive is the weakness of the opposition and as such, you'll gain the advantage. A strong, dominant perspective eliminates your anxiety and gives you peace of mind. It puts you at ease because your view is from the top of the realm of your own life. Your living experience is no longer mysterious because your view of it is now panoramic. You now have a broad overview, within grand parameters. When on the mountainside, your view of the mountain is limited, regardless of how high upon the mountain you ascend. It's only from the *mountaintop* that you can see the entire mountain.

A strong, dominant perspective makes you proactive. It's what causes you to take the initiative in your life's experiences. It determines what constitutes normal and abnormal, acceptable and unacceptable for you in any given scenario. It reveals what's useful and what isn't in any given scenario. Individuals who possess strong, dominant perspectives establish order. They provide the standards and guidelines in any given scenario.

Embracing an identity other than your personal blessing will cause you to develop a weak, submissive perspective. A weak, submissive perspective is the abdication of manhood. It will negatively affect every aspect of your life. You'll be burdened with worry, anxiety and stress. You'll be particularly susceptible to self-abuse. You'll be particularly vulnerable to haphazard personal behavior. Self-destruction is the inevitable result. The trajectory of your own living experience will be a mystery to you. You'll be insecure, unsteady and unsure. You'll always be at a disadvantage. You'll always be *reactive*. You'll be a slave to arbitrary factors. You'll be intimidated by what you see, hear and sense. Fear and insecurity will dominate all that you do. You may even go insane. You'll be an oak trapped in an ornate flowerpot. Your thoughts won't even be your own. You'll be dominated by the thoughts of others. Instead of reigning on the throne of your own living experience, you'll sit upon the footstool of another's. Others will determine the circumference of your life's reality. The diameter of your thoughts, feelings and behavior will reflect the circumference provided to you by others. You'll be tossed to and fro, depending on the propaganda to which you are exposed at any given moment. Your outlook will always be limited by the arbitrary psychological parameters established by others. You'll have a vicarious relationship with your own life. You'll view your own reality through the eyes of others. You'll esteem yourself based on the preferences—the likes, dislikes and standards of others.

When you operate in a weak, submissive perspective, you'll constantly try to fit in with others. You'll constantly try to live up or down to the standards and expectations of others.

Others will set false, arbitrary and changeable standards that will change as soon as you exceed them. They'll string you along as a horse endlessly chases after an unobtainable carrot. You'll constantly chase the acceptance of others. You'll be ever relegated to providing responses to the real or imagined stimuli projected by others. You'll be preoccupied with what others are saying or thinking about you. Your own emotions will be governed by the thoughts, words and actions of others. You'll compromise your personal integrity. You'll be a slave, actual or virtual, bought and sold by the whims of others. Others will *own* you. In the end, you'll discover the harsh reality that you were expendable all along; your efforts never mattered to them anyway.

The price you pay for operating in an identity other than your personal blessing is too high. No self-respecting person should pay such a price. The price for failing to dominate extreme contradictions through maintaining your identity of victory is huge. Man wasn't created to operate in weak, submissive perspectives. Man wasn't created to view his own life through the eyes of others, through the arbitrary distorted prisms others. The Almighty's favor in your life is inhibited when you insist on operating from weak, submissive perspectives. This is why it is vital that you maintain, to the fullest extent of your ability, your personal blessing, come what may. It's the only thing that guarantees a strong, dominant perspective.

DAVID'S DOMINANT PERSPECTIVE

In the story of David and Goliath, David wasn't at the scene of the battle in the role of a soldier. He was still a youth at the time and was actually in the warzone running an errand for Jesse, his father. David's primary duties during this period of his life were to care for his father's sheep. Goliath, on the other hand, was a fully-grown giant of a man, an experienced man of war and champion of the Philistine army. For many days, he verbally challenged the soldiers of the Israelite army. "Choose you a man for you," Goliath would shout, "and let him come down to me."[39] Goliath's problem, though he didn't realize it, was that David happened to be *present* during one of his diatribes. Not long before this chance encounter, David had received his personal blessing. Inwardly, he was no longer just the shepherd of his father's sheep. He was now in possession of the *ultimate* version of himself. He now possessed his identity of victory: *shepherd of Israel*. He was now shepherd of the Almighty's sheep. As blatantly contradictory as this must have seemed at the time, it was true nonetheless; and David embraced it as such.

Those outside David's immediate family had no idea the prophet Samuel had anointed him with an identity of victory, a personal blessing. It appears his own brothers, some of whom were actually in the army, were not keen on the idea of their youngest brother being *their* shepherd. One of them even questioned David about his presence in the warzone.

---

[39] I SAMUEL 17:8

The army knew nothing of David's personal blessing. King Saul knew nothing of David's personal blessing. General Abner knew nothing of David's personal blessing. Goliath and the Philistine army *certainly* knew nothing of David's personal blessing, or that such a phenomenon even existed. But David came to accept and acknowledge his personal blessing as the truth about himself. He fully embraced the ultimate version of himself. As a result, his *perspective* of Goliath and of the Philistine army was one of strength and dominance. David was weak, vis-à-vis Goliath's physical might, but his *perspective* was strong. As such, the only thing he could perceive was Goliath's weakness.

The professional soldiers—the men constituting the armies of the living God—were paralyzed by fear. They were strong, but their collective perspective was weak. Their perspective of weakness nullified their strengths. All they could perceive were Goliath's strengths. This worked to their disadvantage. His perspective of the Philistine champion paralyzed King Saul himself. King Saul, the commander-in-chief of the Israelite armed forces, was *dominated* by the visually imposing figure of Goliath.

David, however, had a dominant perspective that drove him to *immediate* action. When David heard Goliath's defiance of those over whom he was now shepherd, the elements of his destiny structure catapulted him into a different psychological trajectory than that of anyone else. He had a different trajectory than did King Saul. Indeed, the king had been reduced to offering his own daughter to the man who would kill Goliath, but no one dared; that is, no one but David. David even had a different psychological trajectory than did Abner, the high-ranking general of the armed forces. This is the same Abner later eulogized by David, calling him "a prince and a great man."[40] Abner wasn't inclined, however, to confront Goliath. It appears that he too was paralyzed by fear. But when David looked upon Goliath, the only thing he could perceive was Goliath's glaring weakness: a huge exposed forehead. David's dominant perspective enabled him to exploit Goliath's weakness. Using a sling and a stone, the same tools with which he carried out his duties while protecting his father's sheep, David defended the honor of the armies of the living God, whom Goliath openly defied. After David struck Goliath down with the stone, he ran *toward* Goliath, stood *upon* him and then decapitated him with his own sword. A child killed Goliath with his own sword. A dominant perspective converted the giant's strength, making it his weakness. In life, it's never *what* you see that matters, but always *how* you see it that makes the difference.

Upon killing Goliath, David held up the giant's severed head in the midst of the valley. Seeing this, the Philistine army fled. They likely could've won the battle, but they now deemed themselves wholly inadequate to the task of defeating the Israelite forces. After all, these were men who could patiently bide their time, shun provocation, then "choose" a mere youth from among their civilian population to kill the Philistine champion. Of course, this wasn't the case. David just happened to be in the warzone on an errand. It was a chance encounter. But the Philistine army was unaware of this. The interpretation of events based on their own weak perspective sapped them

---

[40] II SAMUEL 3:38

of their courage. They must've thought to themselves, "If one of their children can so skillfully kill the strongest and most valiant among us, how much more will their men of war do to the rest of us?"

A strong, dominant perspective led to the death of Goliath and to the defeat of the Philistine army. David, just a youth at the time, didn't allow extreme contradictions to dominate him. Instead, he dominated extreme contradictions by remaining true to the *ultimate* version of himself in spite of outward appearances; he was victorious as a result.

The ability to dominate extreme contradictions is what catapulted David into the glory of his destiny. So shall it be for you if you will embrace and maintain *fully* your personal blessing at all times. Do not underestimate the greatness of what is happening to and through you at this time. In spite of all contradiction and opposition, remain true to the ultimate version of you. If you do, that version will be true to you. Among multiple other things, your personal blessing will provide you with an indomitable triumphant perspective.

6

THE
NATURE OF
THE FIGHT

"And they shall fight against thee; but they shall not prevail against thee . . ."

—Jeremiah 1:19

TRANSITION OPPOSITION

When you transition into your personal blessing, there will be vicious opposition, much of it from unexpected quarters. You'll experience opposition from your own social group. You'll even experience it from friends and family. Those closest to you will be the first to sense a change in your disposition; they'll be the first to resist the spirit of your personal blessing. You'll be loved, accepted and embraced as long as you remain in your degraded place. In many cases, the self-esteem of others depends on a degraded version of you. They're depending on your minimization. They have a stake in your degradation, an interest in your mediocrity. Your degradation and mediocrity actually makes them feel better about themselves. Your elevated aura agitates those closest to you because you're rejecting what they're depending on to solidify their own self-worth. You're rejecting the role they're expecting you to play. You're no longer providing the sorry image that once marked the boundaries of their own shallow sense of self.

Your transition into your personal blessing can be filled with personal anguish, confusion and frustration. The ultimate version of you is inconsistent with anything others expect of you. The blessing experience can be disconcerting. Much of your opposition won't be direct; it will come at oblique angles. Some of the opposition will shock you. Some of it will break your heart when you discover precisely who's depending on your loss.

The most unlikely individuals are depending on your destruction. There are segments of society that have perverse incentives to stifle and inhibit your positive progress. There are segments of society that benefit from your bondage to something, somewhere or someone. There are segments of society that benefit from your vices and addictions. There are segments of society whose livelihoods depend on the degradation and suffering of others. There are segments of society that benefit from your marginalization. These same insidious segments will vehemently oppose the spirit of your personal blessing. In some way, you'll *sense* their opposition, whether you *see* it or not.

When you shine in your identity of victory, you become an anomaly to others. You are something peculiar, abnormal, not easily classified. Your personal blessing causes you to stand out among the rest. There will be individuals who resent this. The energy with which you shine contradicts what they expect or even want from you. You offend their sensibilities by defying their sensual or historical interpretation of the way things ought to be, concerning you or those like you. Some are as committed to viewing you negatively as you are to embracing your personal blessing. They can't perceive you higher without perceiving themselves lower. This is why they immediately respond so negatively to the spirit of your personal blessing. The more you shine in the glory of your personal blessing, the more animosity you'll receive from them. This dynamic accompanies the blessing territory and goes back thousands of years.

The ancient story of Joseph, son of Jacob, speaks poignantly of the hatred that arises from the unwillingness of some to accept the glory of another. According to the story, Joseph's older brothers "hated him, and could not speak peaceably unto him."[41] Joseph's lofty visions for his own life defied what his brothers were willing accept about him. The more Joseph shared his dreams, the more his brothers hated him. It wasn't that he was doing anything wrong. The problem was that his personal vision cast him higher than his brothers were willing to accept. "Behold," they said to one another, "this dreamer cometh. Come now therefore, and let us slay him . . ."[42]

Individuals who assess you through their own pre-established lens of negativity have a spiritual disease: the hater virus. This virus causes them to become full-blown haters. It's a virus rooted in jealousy, envy and personal insecurity. Those infected with the hater virus had the infection before they encountered you. It only develops into full-blown hate when those infected are exposed to a level of glory that defies their preconceived notions of what ought and ought not to be concerning others. This is why some will hate you for no apparent reason. But your haters don't hate you because they *don't* understand what you're about; they hate you because they understand *exactly* what you're about; they simply can't stand viewing *you* on that level. Haters have an inherent ability to detect glory, because they actually *rely* on glory. Without the glory of others, haters simply have nothing for which to live. This is why haters recognize your glory as soon as they're exposed to it; make no mistake about this.

The greatest danger the hater virus poses is for the *hated* to be infected. If infected by the hater virus, you'll be intimidated out of your own glory and your own glorious destiny. Infection

---

[41]   GENESIS 37:4
[42]   GENESIS 37:19-20

will cause you to minimize and degrade yourself in an effort to reconcile or satisfy the warped sensibilities of others. You'll define yourself through the eyes of others. Self-hatred is the result of contracting the hater virus. Once infected, not only will you begin to hate yourself, but you too will be among those filled with jealousy, envy and personal insecurity. The hater virus is contagious; immunity comes by way of understanding it and remaining true to your identity of victory, no matter what.

THE DANGER OF FITTING IN

You must not commit yourself to pursuing acceptance by others. All too often, you're only acceptable when you're second-rate, living up or down to twisted expectations. You're only acceptable when you're advancing someone else's agenda better than they do themselves. You're only acceptable when you present yourself to be less than you truly are. You're only acceptable when you're broken, defeated and subservient, fully compliant to the destructive designs and expectations of others. You're only acceptable at the bottom, perversely entertaining, tickling the fancies of others. You're only acceptable when others can exploit your gift and make a better living from your pockets than from their own. You're only acceptable when you're *invisible*, when the glorious version of your humanity is blurred. You're only acceptable on drugs, in jail or dead prematurely. You're only acceptable when your integrity is compromised in some wretched way.

In your effort to reconcile the low estimation others have of you, you'll minimize, diminish and degrade yourself. In your effort to fit in, you'll become a shell of the person you were created to be. You'll self-destruct. You'll be like a lion trying to fit in with alley cats, a swan trying to fit in with ducks, an eagle trying to fit in with sparrows. It's not a question of whether you can fit in with others, but always a question of whether others can fit in with you. You're the centerpiece of your life's reality. If you don't have an indomitable sense of self, you'll be vulnerable to everything and everyone. You must live confidently and not be infected with or intimidated by the negative thoughts or words of others. Your personal blessing is doing something extraordinary through you, and others are not the gateway to your legitimacy, nor can they ever be.

Throughout the world, human groups have ways of displaying social displeasure with their respective constituents. In order to express displeasure with the spirit of an individual's disposition, groups and societies will use isolation, alienation, disregard, silence and mistreatment. The mere threat of being labeled an outcast is very effective in keeping people in line. The methods employed by any group are intended to dissuade deviation from what is deemed acceptable. Groups and societies have interests in guiding—sometimes *controlling*—the thoughts and behavior of their members. Social groups have interests in maintaining the social and psychological structures upon which they are based. They have interests in maintaining a particular social scheme or scale, a certain perspective from which they believe all lives should be lived.

I once observed a group-exercise intended to demonstrate the power of social approval and disapproval on the behavior of individuals. Two members of a group of about 20 were asked to step outside a room in which everyone was seated. Their two seats were removed from the circle, preventing them from reclaiming their places upon re-entry. In their absence, the other members decided on some arbitrary but simple act they wished the isolated members to perform when they returned to the room. Group members were to *clap* in approval whenever the two members came even remotely close to engaging in the desired act. No words were to be spoken at all. The objective was to influence their behavior gradually through a universally acknowledged expression of social approval. Group members were instructed to hold their applause whenever the two outcast members deviated or strayed from what was desired of them. Anything they did that was unassociated with what was desired was met with cold silence.

One of the most remarkable aspects of this exercise was that members of the group didn't have to verbalize their expectations in order to convey them. In the absence of verbal cues, the two outcast members immediately caught on to the fact that there were acceptable and unacceptable patterns of behavior in this scenario. Clapping alone was enough to convey this message. But only when clapping was introduced as a stimulus in this exercise did it have the power to influence behavior. It was only when clapping was introduced that stone silence was given any substantive meaning. By reinforcing acceptable behavior using a universally recognized expression of approval, these two outcast members were *pressured* to play along—and play along they did. Eventually, after several minutes of trial and error, the two members actually performed the desired act. By that point, I should add, the clapping had crescendoed into a resounding standing ovation.

In the same way, individuals are manipulated and coerced by elements within their own societies. They are cajoled and maneuvered into embracing certain identities and engaging in certain behaviors. Expectations are woven into the fabrics of societies and the masses are vulnerable to them. But this kind of vulnerability is dangerous, because people can be set up to self-destruct. This is why nothing must trump the primacy of your identity of victory, the primacy of the *ultimate* version of you. Stand to it, though every level and aspect of society would have you to be less. Be true to the ultimate version of you, no matter what.

IDENTITY BOYCOTT

There are many ways others may express approval or disapproval of your personal disposition. The problem is that there are ways of living that may meet the approval of others but that are wholly inconsistent with the ultimate version of you. If you can be pressured by the expectations, approval or disapproval of others, you are also vulnerable to self-destruction.

The 20th century Civil Rights Movement in the United States put to use a powerful method of expressing social disapproval: *the boycott*. A boycott is to engage in a concerted refusal to have dealings with a person, store or organization, usually to express disapproval or to force acceptance of certain conditions. A boycott is really a war of wills. Pressure is the objective. In the context of the Civil Rights Movement, the boycott objective was social, political and economic pressure. As it turns out, the boycott strategy was very effective. Many concessions were gained and significant progress made due to successful boycotts.

Your personal blessing will cause you to defy what is expected of you. The spirit of what you are will challenge the established structures of your present social reality. You'll defy the social orders of your group and of the reality your society projects. You'll defy stigmas, expectations and stereotypes. You'll defy your environment. Your environment has been interpreted in certain ways, and everyone in that context of reality is expected to think and behave according to that interpretation. While operating in your personal blessing, you'll defy the visual interpretations of others. You'll defy established standards and will no longer embrace your previous degraded place. Others will sense the change in your disposition. Others will boycott the spirit of your personal blessing. The boycotting of your identity is intended to pressure you. An identity-boycott is an evil proposition; it's social intimidation, social seduction of the most insidious sort. The message is, "Until you come to your *senses* and get back down where you belong, you won't be recognized, respected or even acknowledged." An identity-boycott is intended to make you *persona non grata*; it sends the message that you don't even exist; that you're invisible and that you don't matter. You'll be isolated, alienated and ostracized until you give in to the demands of the boycotters.

The war of life is a war for your personal identity. Never forget this. The identity boycott is a blatant act of war. The fight for your personal identity is a dirty war. If you *can* be intimidated, you *will* be. You must maintain the integrity of your personal blessing, no matter what. The strategy of the opposition is to get you to compromise the integrity of your personal blessing.

The identity boycott is really an indication of something wonderful. It's an affirmative indication that you're shining with the glory of your victorious identity. It's evidence that your life has been restructured; that it has taken a different trajectory, a different course. Absolute personal integrity is required of you. Obedience in the face of cruel opposition is required of you. You don't deserve the manifestation of your vision if you can't withstand the onslaught of the opposition. In the face of vicious opposition, declare unto thyself, "This is *my* personal blessing, the ultimate version of *me*, and I have the right to live *in* it. What others think I should be makes no difference to me."

THE WAR

The main thing of which you must constantly be aware is that you are in a war for your personal identity. Your personal blessing isn't going to blossom uncontested; it will be tried by fire. Living in your personal blessing is a struggle between good and evil. It's a struggle of epic proportions, with life and death implications. You must understand the nature of any fight in which you're a combatant. It's possible to be ready, willing and able to fight, but still *lose* the fight. You can lose by simply failing to understand the *nature* of the fight. Superior armies have lost battles and wars because they didn't understand the nature of the fight in which they were involved.

Suspects placed under arrest in certain regions of the world have a set of rights read to them. A general reading of their rights informs them of the *nature* of their fight: "You have a right to remain silent. If you give up that right, anything you say can and will be used against you in the court of law . . ." Many times suspects give up their right to silence. They choose to speak, believing their words will only help them out of trouble. But as many convicted felons will testify, the next time they heard their own words, repeated by the public prosecutor in court, those words were cleverly twisted and being used *against* them.

THE 6-POINT CHECKLIST

It's vital that you be clear on the nature of any fight, struggle or personal war in which you are a combatant. Ignorance may cost more than you're able to pay. The way to understand the nature of any fight or struggle in which you're involved is the 6-point checklist. You need to know who, what, when, where, how and why.

The first thing you must know is *who* the enemy or opponent is. An awareness of who the enemy is will give you insight into his nature. You must understand his history and become aware of his background. This will expose you to your enemy's tendencies. You'll come to understand his identity, how he thinks, along with the rest of his destiny structure.

The second thing you need to know is *what* the fight is over. You need to be ever conscious of what is at stake. Only then will you understand the implications of winning and losing. You need to know what your enemy or opponent is really after. What is his objective? What is his aim? What constitutes victory in his mind? By understanding the enemy's objective, you can formulate coherent strategies and methods that will enable you to countervail his efforts. You can thwart and frustrate the enemy through proper preparation when you know exactly what the prize is. You can develop uniquely effective methods and strategies when you have a firm grasp of what the fight is all about.

The third thing you must know is *when* the fight occurs. Timing in any battle is critical. If you're not conscious of the timing of the fight, you can be taken unawares; you can be ambushed. Knowing the timing of the fight keeps you vigilant and alert. It enables you to develop a timetable for preparation. It also enables you to develop the appropriate pace for your operations. Having correct timing enables you to undermine the well thought-out plans and strategies of the enemy. You'll be able to anticipate the enemy's operation. You'll always be two and three steps ahead of what the enemy is devising. His *fastest* move will be far too slow.

The fourth thing you must know is *where* the fight is. What constitutes the battlefield in your fight? Are you familiar with the battlefield? Knowing the parameters of the battlefield puts you at ease, empowering you to maneuver effectively. Effective planning requires battlefield knowledge. The more familiar you are with the battlefield, the greater your advantage. It's possible to be in a war, but not fighting the war at the appropriate front. Your focus may be on one location, yet the critical battle in another. You need to know where the critical fight is.

The fifth thing you need to know is *how* the fight is being conducted. Being aware of how the fight is fought enables you to prepare effectively. You'll be able to debunk the enemy's methods if you understand the way the fight is being waged. You'll devise methods that give you the advantage when you know exactly how the battle is being conducted. Knowing how the fight is being fought enables you to assess your own strengths and weaknesses. It enables you to build yourself up in areas that may not be as strong as are other areas.

The sixth and final thing you must know is *why* the fight is being waged. Why is what's at stake worth fighting for? Understanding why the fight is being engaged exposes you to the history of the struggle. It brings into sharp focus what the opponent's motives are. Knowing why the fight is being fought gives you insight into the psychological focus of the enemy. You'll understand what the enemy's inspiration really is. You'll then be able to regulate the intensity of your operations more skillfully.

The 6-point checklist applies to any kind of fight, war, battle, contest or competition. Most importantly, the checklist is vital for the man who is in possession of his personal blessing. Let's explore them in order.

WHO

In order to succeed in the extraordinary lifestyle called for by the sacred formula, you must realize that you have an enemy. Satan is the enemy, and he uses human operatives. He uses people as his minimizing, degrading, dehumanizing cat's claws. Satan is well aware of the power of personal identity. After all, he hasn't always been Satan, the adversary. He was "Lucifer, son of the morning!"[43] He's very familiar with the identity-change phenomenon because he is a fallen angel who experienced it himself. The wickedness and evil he envisioned required that he abandon the identity of *Lucifer* in exchange for the identity of *Satan*. Lucifer couldn't actually produce wickedness, but Satan could—and he did. Lucifer corrupted and twisted the power of identity-change within his own living experience. He understands very well the Law of Destiny and Law of Human Nature. He understands the blessing formula. He isn't under any illusions about the power of the blessing phenomenon.

WHAT

The prize in this fight is your self-concept, your self-perception, your self-definition, your self-truth. As I mentioned, the enemy understands this divine information better than most people do. This is why he has worked so cleverly to obscure these profound principles throughout the centuries. The enemy

---

[43]   ISAIAH 14:12

knows you have the ability and the right to *choose* your own personal identity, thereby governing your own destiny.

Satan is a focused entity. He is after something very specific. He's after your personal identity. He's after what you accept and acknowledge as the truth about yourself—*inwardly*. Again, the enemy isn't under any illusions. He knows that when your vision manifests, not only will it bless your life, but it will bless the lives of others as well. This is why his ultimate aim is to sidetrack that destiny. But the only way he can do that is to attack and subdue your destiny's source—your personal identity. His sole objective is to seize control of and corrupt the identity aspect of your mind.

The enemy is in the identity business. The main aim of his business is to distribute his product. He has an entire collection of minimized, degraded, situational identities from which he would have you to choose. The enemy wants to expose you to the full range of his options. He wants you to feel good about selecting any identity he offers. He wants you to be comfortable with your choice of minimized self-concepts. You should know, however, that all of the enemy's identities are demeaning and destructive. His desire is to cheapen you. He wants to diminish and depreciate you in your *own* sight. The enemy wants all divine human greatness subdued and muted. He wants to influence the human spirit and condition in ways of minimization and destruction. This is why the blessing and the blessed are always Satan's archenemies.

WHEN

You are under *constant* attack by the enemy. Situations, circumstances, environments, events and others are constantly saying something to you, about you. They are constantly suggesting and implying things to you, about you. By surrounding you with sensory propaganda of all sorts, remaining in attack mode, the enemy seeks to undermine your stability by catching you at a vulnerable moment. This is why there can be no "down-time" for the blessed man. You must be ever vigilant. You must be wholeheartedly committed to remaining in the spirit of your personal blessing at all times.

WHERE

The battlefield in this war is within your own mind. The identity dimension of your mind is the focal point, the precise theatre of combat. You must be aware of any tendencies to drift away from or lose focus on *what* you are. Being aware of your own identity tendencies and proclivities enables you to gauge the amount of repetitive elevating self-talk you require on a daily or momentary basis. You must understand the battlefield fully. Focus on the identity aspect of your own mind by acknowledging your personal blessing constantly and consistently. The identity aspect of your own mind is where the fight is; it's the theatre of combat you must dominate.

HOW

The enemy never intended for you to arrive at this glorious phase of your being. He did everything he could to sabotage your journey. He did everything he could to permanently minimize and degrade you. He wanted you permanently traumatized and shaken. But in the end, his efforts failed miserably. You'd think his failure would cause him to abort his mission, but that's exactly what he wants *you* to do. He's depending on extreme contradictions to intimidate you out of your personal blessing. He's depending on the powerful dynamics of human conditioning, on the natural desire for the things of life to correspond to intimidate you out of your personal blessing. He wants nothing more than for you to abandon your personal blessing in frustration. He wants you to conform. He wants you to devalue yourself. He wants you to relinquish your personal blessing to the outward appearance of things.

The enemy wants you to fit into that which is being projected around you by him and his operatives. He's depending on overwhelming contradictory propaganda to lower your personal morale and break you down. His strategy is to bombard you with all kinds of situations, circumstances, environments, events, people, pressure, stereotypes, expectations, scenarios, distractions, attitudes, mistreatment, confusing messages and uncertainty. He wants to turn you into a broken-down zombie, a despicable product of select combinations of everything going on around you. The enemy wants to *overwhelm* you to the extent that you give up and define yourself based on all the madness with which you're being bombarded. The enemy wants to cause social insanity, if not clinical insanity, for you in this life.

If you define yourself based on outside factors, your life will in fact reproduce the substance and spirit of those factors in your future, beginning right now. Your life will produce a vicious cycle of defeat, because it will be a product of twisted shallow social propaganda. This is what the enemy wants for your life. Your life has no choice but to conform to the *nature* of your self-concept. Understand that a personal identity based on arbitrary factors is a curse. Your hope will be one thing, but your life will produce something completely different. The enemy wants you to be overcome, shaken and insecure. He wants you to internalize that with which you are being bombarded. He wants you to pollute and dilute your personal identity. He wants you to corrupt your life with demeaning degrading thoughts about yourself. He wants you to submit to the pressure of arbitrary factors.

The enemy will use any and all methods to steer you away from operating in the spirit of the ultimate version of you. He will use intimidation, temptation, seduction, habits, trickery and even violence. He will use your history: what you did; what you said; what happened to you and so on. He'll use his human operatives to undermine strategically and deceptively your personal identity. The presence of those who are complicit in the enemy's tactics is intended ultimately to affect negatively the way you define *yourself*. You will hear offensive things said to and about you, whether audibly or inaudibly. You'll also experience dismissive attitudes and mistreatment.

The enemy wants you to believe that the identities he offers by way of his propaganda are the only legitimate identities from which to choose. He wants to discredit the uniquely elevated identity revealed to you through your personal blessing. Instead, he wants you to *abandon* your personal blessing and come to feel that it's somehow a privilege to possess one of *his* identities. He wants you to take pride in the situational identity *he's* provided for you. In this way, you'll be seduced into holding it dear. You'll actually defend a degrading personal identity; it'll be *precious* in your sight. The enemy wants to give you the impression that you've *earned* one of his degraded identities. He wants to give you the impression that you've somehow been *elevated* to a higher status or station through what is actually a minimizing identity. This is why the enemy confronts you so viciously with daunting, contradictory scenarios. By overwhelming you, the enemy is saying, "Pick one of these appropriate situational identities. Choose an identity that reflects the obvious situation of your life. You see what the outward circumstances are. Just keep it real and *conform* to what you see. Anything less is ridiculous." In this way, the enemy wants to be the gateway to your "legitimacy." If he achieves his will, you'll be easily manipulated and readily reined in. His idea is for you to get into the habit of defining yourself based on arbitrary factors. In this way, you'll be brought low, kept off balance and forever contained, controlled like a puppet on strings.

But don't be deceived by the allure of any situational personal identity. There are things in every man's life that simply must not be compromised. The fullness of manhood, honor and nobility, as it relates to the *ultimate* version of you, are non-negotiable.

The enemy's identities do nothing but make you fuel for his fire. They dehumanize you in the most wicked fashion, because while they may seem like normal, even prestigious identities, they're not. They're actually intended to stifle and smother the greatness the Most High has placed within you.

The activation of your personal blessing is the enemy's worst nightmare come true. It's among the worst things that could happen to him. This is why he despises the *ultimate version* of you so much. The ultimate version of you exposes the enemy's versions of you for what they really are—limiting destructive organisms.

Your personal blessing also obliterates the enemy's projected walls of reality. Your personal blessing shatters the enemy's cognitive contexts of reality. This is why your personal blessing is such a threat to the enemy. As divine contagion, your personal blessing is out of the enemy's control. It inspires life in the very persons he's looking to limit and destroy. Control, subjugation and human destruction are the enemy's obsessions. Your personal blessing denies him his desire. This is why he will use all means at his disposal in a vain attempt to bring you under his control. You'll sense vicious hostility and cruel animosity from the enemy's operatives. This is intended to intimidate you. The enemy wants you to feel insecure, out of place and isolated. He wants you to feel unbearable loneliness.

Your personal blessing freed you from bondage, and set you on the course of experiencing the highest possible level of freedom available to you. Once you embraced your personal blessing, the enemy could only aim at getting you to doubt yourself and abort the process. But only *you* can re-enslave yourself by abandoning the ultimate truth about yourself.

You are far greater than the enemy wants you to be. He never wanted you exposed to the *ultimate* version of you. He never wanted you to realize it. The enemy never wanted you to receive the blessing formula or understand the Law of Destiny and the Law of Human Nature. His objective was to keep you *far* from the only phenomenon in the world that could and would guarantee freedom at its highest level. Satan never intended for you to know that you were independently wonderful—independently great. He never wanted you to be exposed to the *ultimate* dimension of your existence. Instead, he wanted you eating out of his hand like a trained animal. He wanted you psychologically drinking his personality-warping poisonous identities until they destroyed you. The enemy wanted you dependent upon him so he could continue playing with your life like rag-doll—like a cat toys with its prey before the kill. The enemy never wanted you to be independent of your situations; independent of your circumstances; independent of your environments, independent of events and nefarious social mechanisms. He wanted you as his human bonsai, so he could truncate, control, restrict and usurp whatever abilities you bring to the table for his own wicked ends.

The most devastating thing in the world is to be subject to the enemy. It's similar but worse than being married to a batterer. The enemy wants to keep you in a perpetual state of Battered Human Syndrome. He wants the ability to traumatize and destabilize you at any given moment through situational, circumstantial and environmental triggers. He wants you completely under his control. But the only way to control you is to control your *personal identity*. The enemy wants to prostitute you psychologically. He wants to be your identity-pimp. But you don't need the enemy's situational, circumstantial or environmentally based identities to legitimize *your* living experience. You don't need to defile yourself to please the sensibilities of the enemy or his operatives, wearing his identity like a cheap short skirt. Your personal blessing is more legitimate than anything the enemy has to offer to you. In fact, your personal blessing is *more* legitimate than the enemy is himself, and the identities he offers are even less legitimate than he is. Every identity the enemy has to offer is warped, degrading and destructive. Your personal blessing, on the other hand, is the favor of the Almighty bestowed upon your life. The same can't be said for Satan's personal identity.

<u>WHY</u>

Satan is in rebellion against the good the Most High wills for man upon the earth. From the beginning, he's possessed some misguided, demented desire to compete with his Creator. The reason the enemy wants to undermine your personal identity is that he understands the implications of your dream coming true. He understands that your victory will greatly inspire others. The lives of humans will be blessed for many generations to come because of the glory that accompanies the manifestation of your vision. His only hope was to keep you ignorant of the fact that there *was* an ultimate version of you *available* to you. As long as he could keep you preoccupied with arbitrary elements and their corresponding identities, he never had to be concerned with you realizing that there was far more to you than you were experiencing.

When the blessing of Abraham has saturated the living, humanity will realize a version of itself never before imagined. The enemy wants to stave off this experience—this epoch of human history—as long as he can, for he knows that his time is short.

WINNING YOUR FIGHT

The key is for you to be "stedfast, unmoveable, always abounding"[44] in your personal blessing, which is the "work of the Lord" in your life. It is acceptable to walk away from certain fights. Some fights are simply not worth the trouble. But there are other fights that absolutely must be engaged. The fight to solidify your personal blessing as your personal identity is such a case. The fight for your personal blessing must be engaged. There is no greater victory than winning the fight for the *ultimate* version of you. Winning this fight is indicative of the highest freedom and *mastery* of the Law of Destiny and the Law of Human Nature. This victory is so rewarding because the opposition to it is so great. In truth, opposition to your living experience has always been at issue, but possessing your personal blessing arouses the viciousness of the opposition like never before. This is why your identity of victory must

---

[44] I CORINTHIANS 15:58

be *invincible*. Everything in your life must be *relative* to your personal blessing. Your identity of victory is permanent. It's like the sun around which all else orbits. Relate to everything and everyone from the perspective of your personal blessing. Don't budge, compromise or give in—*ever*. Let the chips fall where they may, and accept the wonderful outcome.

Experience your life in full from the grand perspective of your personal blessing. Situations and circumstances come and go; environments and people change; individuals and seasons come and go. Life changes in unpredictable ways. Keep your personal blessing steady, indomitable, impenetrable and invulnerable. It must be protected, defended and stood for at all costs. How? By remaining true to it at all times. Shine *brightly* with the glory of your personal blessing at all times. The greatest personal testimony a man can give upon the earth is, "I won the war for my personal blessing; it is settled. I'm now operating in the *ultimate version* of me. I'm now the undisputed champion of my own life for the rest of my life, and it's a beautiful thing!"

You can lose everything, but if you preserve your personal blessing, you will have really lost *nothing*. On the other hand, you can gain everything, but lose your victorious identity, and you will have actually lost *everything*. Any man who has not redefined himself in the present based on his own vision of his victorious future is a *slave* to something, somewhere or someone. One thing is for sure, he is *not* free. He may be in the *midst* of freedom, but something, somewhere or someone binds him. He is a situational zombie, subject and subservient to the ever-changing factors of the world around him.

It's better to be free in the midst of bondage than to be bound in the midst of freedom. It's better to victorious in the midst of defeat than defeated in the midst of victory. Always your life produces according to *what* you are and not where you are. You now know the nature of this fight. Knowing what you now know, you must reign triumphantly in the *ultimate version* of you at all times. In this is your victory!

7

WHAT
NOW?

"For the vision is yet for an appointed time, but at the end it shall speak, and not lie: though it tarry, wait for it; because it will surely come . . ."

—Habakkuk 2:3

THE NECESSITY OF A VISION

The man endowed with the blessing formula must first have a *vision* for his own life. Vision always precedes mission. It's always easy to identify a God-given vision, dream or goal because when it manifests, not only will it bless the visionary, but it will bless everyone else too. God-given visions are to the *benefit* of others, not at their *expense*. People don't suffer from the manifestation of a God-given vision. It's always a win-win proposition when a God-given dream manifests, because it brings out the best in everyone. Abram had such a vision and so do you.

There is a reason that you have the personal vision that you have. The purpose of your personal vision is to reveal what your life can and ought to produce upon the earth. If for no other reason, respect your vision for *that*. Your vision provides you with something for which to live. Your manifested vision will bless the lives of others, just as the manifested visions of others have blessed your life, though you knew nothing of their visions until they were manifest.

"Where there is no vision, the people perish . . ."[45] It's a well-established fact that having a personal vision for your future is life sustaining. There is more to a thriving life on earth than food, shelter and clothing. Having no *vision* for the future of your life is deadly. Not only does the lack of a vision deprive you of something for which to live, it deprives you of the very thing from which you must extract the element that can *produce* anything. Without a vision, you'll be aimless, tossed about by

---

[45] PROVERBS 29:18

the ever-changing winds of time and circumstance. Without a vision, you'll be vulnerable to everything. There's nothing you may or may not do.

Austrian psychiatrist Viktor Frankl, whose mother, father, brother and pregnant wife were killed in Nazi concentration camps was able to survive his own captivity by *believing* that a special task awaited him in life. Many imprisoned in Nazi death camps died literally of broken hearts—severe depression—a condition known as fixed melancholy. Dr. Frankl was able to *help* fellow inmates summon the will to live by finding some personal meaning for their own lives. He encouraged them to live *for* something, something contradicting the dire situation in which they found themselves. In this way, they were able to sustain the *spirit of life* in the midst of unspeakable death. Dr. Frankl's analysis was that the underlying need of human existence is to find *meaning* in life. In his most famous work, *Man's Search for Meaning: An introduction to Logotherapy,* Dr. Frankl summed up his conclusions by explaining, "Man does not simply exist, but always decides what his existence will be, what he will become in the next moment."[46] This truth, of course, corresponds with the Law of Human Nature: *Identity Selectivity.* Dr. Frankl concluded that man always has the ability to *choose* his own self-definition, no matter what. He was correct. Man has the ability and the right to *select* his own personal identity, based on the past, present *or* his vision of the future.

---

[46] Viktor Frankl, *Man's Search for Meaning:* An Introduction to Logotherapy (1962; translated into English, 1970) pg. 206.

We now know that individuals fare better in life when they have self-definitions based on their visions of their victorious future. People are better off when they have something for which to live, something in the future they're looking forward to doing or achieving. During the years of the European slave trade of Africans, it became common knowledge among slave traders that Bushmen, a culture indigenous to southern Africa, were of a disposition that would cause them to actually *will* themselves to death rather than suffer removal from their ancient way of life, which was the *hope* of their lives. Slavers wouldn't waste their time attempting to seize Bushmen. As it turned out, other African cultures were more amenable to slavery because they were peoples who had cultivated the ability to maintain *hope*, beyond current realities. For these peoples, *hopelessness* was not an option.

As we understand it today, hopelessness is a deadly spiritual and mental health issue. Among those serving significant prison terms, individuals who maintain a *hope* for the future fare better in terms of physical and mental health than do those who resign themselves to the dreary contexts of prison walls. Hopelessness among the incarcerated causes them to become sullen, lifeless and, in far too many cases, mentally ill. Suicides are common among the incarcerated. Mental deterioration and premature death are common occurrences among those incarcerated for lengthy periods.

There are horror stories of long-term prison inmates who went insane and died after being told they would be released on a certain day, only to have their hopes shattered by a last minute decision to rescind their release and extend indefinitely their sentence. Indeed, there are modern penal systems that are notorious for this sordid practice. Authorities do this purposely, in an effort to crush the spirits and hopes of these persons and their expectant family members. Humans require something to look forward to, without which they will die mentally—then physically.

MANDELA

The great Nelson Mandela was able to step out of his prison cell and directly into the presidential palace after 27 years of imprisonment. This was possible because he never relinquished the noble vision he had for his life. No matter what, he maintained a *vision* of victory and the *identity* of victory extracted from it. He never relinquished his personal identity to what were daunting situations, circumstances, environments and events, all of which were out of his control. He couldn't control sadistic prison officials or their skewed perspectives of him. Though he certainly wept many a night, Madiba (Mandela's family name) surely read the poignant verse of David's psalm: "He that goeth forth and weepeth, bearing precious seed, shall doubtless come again with rejoicing, bringing his sheaves with him."[47] Remember, your personal blessing is *precious* seed.

---

[47] PSALMS 126:6

IMAGINATION

Your imagination is just as important as your vision is. In fact, your imagination is vital to your vision. The imagination-aspect of your mind is extremely valuable mental real estate. It's this aspect of your mind that enlivens and vivifies your vision. Your imagination customizes your vision; it personalizes it. Your imagination is what makes your vision uniquely yours. Accordingly, your imagination can work for or against you. If you have an identity of defeat, your imagination will still do what it's designed to do. It will customize and personalize your *defeated* destiny structure. It will enliven and vivify your own defeat. It will make a destructive life even more real and personal. You'll end up embracing vivid self-destruction as your unique customized way of life. You'll actually feel that destruction *belongs* to you.

On the other hand, your imagination works to your advantage when you operate in your personal blessing. You'll begin to personalize a victorious life in ways that only you can. You'll begin to customize your vision in ways that bear witness to the unique individual you are. Remember, when it comes to personal identity, *real* is whatever you select as your personal identity; it's your choice; your imagination just makes it *more* real and personal.

THE CURSE VS. THE BLESSING

Many of us are familiar with the elements of the curse through personal experience and observation. We know how a pervasive sense of despair, distress, heartbreak, disappointment and loss looks and feels. We know how bondage and destruction looks and feels. We thought constant turmoil and tragedy in our lives were just how life was. It's all we knew, and we had gotten used to it. We hoped better times would come along someday, but what we *didn't* know was that what we were seeing and experiencing was in fact the manifestation of the curse. Biblically, it's called the "curse of the law."[48] No one wants to be cursed. No one intends to be cursed. Most would end their cursed experience if they only could. But how can you end something you can't even identify? God's "people are gone into captivity, because they have no knowledge . . ."[49] They are "destroyed for lack of knowledge . . ."[50] Knowledge of particular information is the key. Something that God's people don't *know* is causing them to experience bondage and destruction. There are things you need to *know*. You must be taught about the blessing and the curse.

Both the blessing and the curse have *one* thing in common. They are both identity-based phenomena. They are, at their cores, *identities*—destiny seeds. But this is where the commonality ends. The blessing and the curse are two different *types* of seed, producing completely different effects. They

---

48 GALATIANS 3:13
49 ISAIAH 5:13
50 HOSEA 4:6

are diametrically opposite types of seed. They represent two completely different dimensions of life. It's impossible to be blessed *and* cursed at the same time. You're experiencing either one dimension or the other. Understanding the curse actually helps you to gain a greater understanding of the blessing. As we've already discussed, the blessing of Abraham, which is the operative blessing in this text, is the identity of victory extracted from your vision of victory but embraced in the present with absolute confidence.

The "curse of the law," however, is the identity of defeat extracted from some arbitrary situation, circumstance or environment but embraced in the present with absolute confidence. Whereas the blessing is the ultimate, greatest and most wonderful version of you, the curse is a distorted version of you. It's a twisted, mutated, low-grade version of you. Whereas the blessing produces the *highest* possible living experience available to you, the curse produces the *lowest* possible living experience available to you. The blessing produces victory, fulfillment and peace of mind in every aspect of life. The curse produces defeat, emptiness and despair in every aspect of life. The blessing is to the *benefit* of others, while the curse is always at the *expense* of others.

GENERATIONAL CURSES

There are generations of families infected with the "curse of the law." Families of every sort are infected with the curse:

nuclear families; extended families; cultural families; national families and even spiritual families.

Generational curses by definition are passed from one generation to the next. A generational curse is multiple generations of the same family embracing personal identities of defeat. It's when multiple generations of the same family are exposed to the lowest possible living experiences available to them; when multiple generations of the same family know nothing but a cycle of defeat, emptiness and despair, which ultimately leads to bondage and destruction. Children born into generational curses are shaped and molded by their families' dysfunctions. They become parts, unique dimensions, of their families' curses. These children come to personalize and customize their own curses—their own distorted personal identities—to fit their inherited dysfunctions. Their own imaginations work against them. Curses seem normal for the individuals born into them. The dysfunctional roles they play in their families are reinforced by others, and come to fit them like gloves. They seem tailor-made just for them.

Children born into generational curses will even become territorial and protective of their own self-destructive positions. While they may resent their peculiar roles, they will nevertheless acknowledge them as their own. The relationships these children have with themselves, others and with the world as a whole are based on distorted versions of themselves. Their identities are blueprinted to produce heartbreak, tragedy and disappointment; they are programmed to produce defeat, emptiness and despair.

It's far too convenient to blame cursed families for lack of discipline or lack of wholesome values. It's important to remember that the generational dents and bruises are not of the making of those who inherited them. Must they accept responsibility for themselves in this world? Absolutely; but it is important to acknowledge that they *inherited* their curses. They were *born* into them. A cursed reality is all they ever knew; but they would end that living experience if they only knew how.

In most cases, the origin of a family's curses dates back many generations to distant traumatic events or circumstances, events painfully inescapable for those originally affected. The effects continue to manifest to this day because one wicked extreme begets another. Ensuing generations aren't the sources of their cursed experience; they represent perpetual *products* of some wretched experience that brutalized the personal identities of *others*.

There are cultural families upon the earth whose entire immediate ancestral lines experienced crushing subjugation of their personal identities. Others dehumanized their entire ancestral lines by violently stripping them of their personal identities. Many years later, their descendants are born particularly vulnerable in the area of personal identity. Because of no cultural event marking recovery, they are susceptible to defining themselves based on *anything*. While personal identity should be the strongest aspect, it's the weakest aspect of their being.

Members of a generationally cursed family don't have to know of or even understand the sources of their family's traumatic experience in order for those sources to continue spawning representative fruit. Current generations don't necessarily *want* to live a cursed existence; they don't *intend* to live a cursed existence. What they lack is *knowledge* of specific information. They lack knowledge of their human inheritance, the blessing formula.

EFFECTIVE LEADERSHIP

In the days of Moses, the Almighty exposed the newly delivered Israelites to their sacred family legacy, which was the blessing of Abraham. Moses was in fact leading them to the land promised to Abraham centuries prior. This is where we get the term *promised land*. The Israelites were a dysfunctional lot, fresh from a gruesome slavery experience. Over a period of a few centuries, they descended from a wealthy, thriving people whose connection to Egypt was predated by Joseph's (*Zaphnath-paaneah's*) royal ascent. They went from the status of royal family to *royal slaves* in a matter of a few generations. The nation was going through a traumatic experience when they struck out on their own—to the land promised to Abraham, Isaac and Jacob. Clearly, they were at the bottom of society in that part of the world at that time. They were an unsettled nation of former slaves moving through the wilderness phase of their history.

But notice that it was against this contradictory backdrop that the Almighty called them "a peculiar treasure unto me above all people . . ."[51] He didn't give them an identity based

---

[51]   EXODUS 19:5

on their past or present situations. Instead, He gave them an identity of victory extracted from their vision of victory, and then commanded them to embrace it in the *present* tense, with absolute confidence. Their responsibility was to embrace faithfully that collective identity of victory in spite of all outward contradictory appearances. Only then could they be what they needed to be. Only then could what needed to come out of them emerge. Only then could they manifest the highest possible living experience available to them—the highest possible level of freedom and liberation available to them. The Almighty required that Moses and the Israelites dominate extreme contradictions by remaining true to their ultimate version: *a peculiar treasure unto God above all other peoples*. It was Moses' job to articulate the identity of his people, and he did just that.

As in the ancient story of Moses, family leadership has a distinct purpose. Regardless of the level, family leadership provides structure, guidance and direction. This is why effective leadership requires both knowledge and wisdom. Every generation will produce its own leadership. When, for whatever reason, there's a *lack* of effective leadership, family groups have no wholesome parameters within which to govern or navigate their living experiences. This is true whether dealing with a small family unit or with an entire nation. Leadership deficiency has particularly negative consequences for peoples who have experienced great identity-crushing trauma, for they will be vulnerable to *everything*.

Moses was an excellent model of family leadership. He led a nation of downtrodden former slaves out of bondage, through the wilderness, to the brink of the Promised Land—the land promised to their patriarch. For them, this was the land of abundant opportunity, the land "flowing with milk and honey."[52] Prior to Moses' death, the Almighty allowed him to ascend Mount Nebo, *the lofty place*, on the outskirts of the land of promise. From this vantage point, Moses was allowed view the whole of the land with his own eyes. This marked the end of Moses' personal role in the mission of God's people. He died on the mountain. Before he died, though, Moses got the opportunity to *warn* his people about their lifestyles upon entering the land of promise. He wrote his exhortation down for posterity's sake. He adamantly warned the children of Israel of the possibility of being cursed in the Promised Land, cursed in the midst of abundant opportunity. He warned them to remain true to what the Almighty had *called* them, no matter what. He warned them that failure to remain true to what God had called them would carry dire consequences. The price for abandoning their identity of victory and embracing others would be high. He told them to "hearken diligently"[53] to the parameters of their unique calling. He made it abundantly clear that they weren't like other nations and shouldn't therefore conduct themselves as such. Moses informed the ancient Israelites that the extent to which they remained faithful to their collective blessing is the extent to which they would be exposed to the highest possible living experience available to them—the highest possible level of freedom and liberation available to them. Having been duly

---

[52] EXODUS 3:8
[53] DEUTERONOMY 28:1

warned, the Israelites entered the Promised Land under the able hand of Joshua.

DR. MARTIN LUTHER KING JR.

We don't have to look far to find more recent parallels to this extraordinary piece of ancient history. Dr. Martin Luther King Jr. was an excellent example of family leadership in the symbolic mold of Moses. King led his people—descendants of enslaved Africans of the Western Hemisphere—from a form of bondage. Using great wisdom, he led them through the wilderness of the Civil Rights Movement to the brink of their Promised Land, their phase of abundant opportunity. In his final speech, Dr. King even used the symbolism of Moses' mountaintop to describe the critical juncture at which he perceived his own people to be. Speaking to a standing-room only crowd at historic Mason Temple in Memphis, Tennessee, from the pulpit of the late great Bishop Charles Harrison Mason, King declared, "I've been to the mountaintop . . . and I've looked over, and I've seen the Promised Land. I may not get there with you, but I want you to know tonight that we as a people will get to the Promised Land . . ."

Where Dr. King symbolically differs from Moses is in the fact that he never got the opportunity to *warn* his people about the hazards—the social, political and spiritual traps—they would encounter in the Promised Land. He was assassinated the day following the mountaintop speech. Symbolically, Dr. King died on the mountain. But this was an unnatural loss of monumental leadership, and no one could adequately fill his shoes; nor could anyone adequately articulate the noble historical path of the descendants of enslaved Africans.

The descendants of enslaved Africans would gradually wander into the Promised Land phase of their history without clearly articulated parameters. They entered the Promised Land phase of their history without a consciousness of how to perpetuate their own culture's agenda. They entered the Promised Land phase of their history without knowledge of the sacred formula and, as a result, began to embody aggressively the agendas of others. They began to embrace the values systems, cultural perspectives and identities of others. It was the equivalent of the ancient Israelites moving into the Promised Land in order to embrace the values and perspectives of the Canaanite populations already living there—people like the Amalekites, Jebusites, Moabites and Ammonites.

The descendants of enslaved Africans even went so far as to attribute the great deliverance of their ancestors from the fiery furnace of slavery to *political* figures and entities rather than to the Almighty. Following centuries of their ancestors' bondage, the descendants of enslaved Africans didn't even set aside a holy day of prayer and thanks to memorialize what the Almighty had done for them. Instead, they gave "pharaoh" credit for what the Most High had performed. This was blasphemy, though to this day, many of them don't even realize it. Owing to the error of their ways, they've been unable to advance effectively their own centuries-long legacy of freedom. Instead, they embrace—some would even say *champion*—the decadent, subversive definitions of freedom brought forth by others. This triggered dire consequences for the descendants of enslaved Africans, laid bare for the entire world to see. Instead of a shining testimony, they became a hissing and a byword. Others pass their way and shake their heads in disgust at the waste.

CURSED IN THE PROMISED LAND

"For where does one run to when he's already in the promised land?"

—Claude Brown,
Manchild in the Promised Land

Today the descendants of enslaved Africans have a world of opportunity before them. They're in the Promised Land phase of their history, the phase "flowing with milk and honey." Everything is accessible to them. They can read, write, go, come, buy, sell, eat at lunch-counters, ride at the front of the bus, drink from fountains, and do everything else they've always wanted to do. They can now live in whatever their money can purchase and occupy the highest political and financial stations of society. Collectively, they have enormous resources. As a group, they're a long way from chattel slavery. They may freely achieve what they will.

But 40 years following the death of Dr. King, his people are facing massive social decay. Current incarceration statistics reveal that those of African descent in the Western Hemisphere haven't been in physical bondage in such high numbers since prior to the Civil War. The Prison Industrial Complex and the cradle-to-cell socio-political programme has become a huge money making enterprise on the backs of descendants of enslaved Africans. Prisons, private and otherwise, are bursting at the seams with them. Some social scientists expect the numbers to grow even larger in the coming years.

In spite of insidiously wretched educational and criminal justice systems, this present-day bondage of Africans in the Western Hemisphere is largely *self*-imposed. Owing to their foolish efforts to assimilate the values and identities brought forth by others, *self*-destruction became prevalent among descendants of enslaved Africans. Today, they are represented out of all proportion to their numbers in every category indicating catastrophic social decay and disintegration. The statistics are overwhelming and heartbreaking. Millions of descendants of enslaved Africans have been born into generational curses, and their lives bear witness.

Because of foolish efforts to assimilate the values of and to embrace the established identities brought forth by others, the descendants of enslaved Africans look *to* others for solutions to their *own* problems and dilemmas. But there are no political or legislative agendas that can break the curses the descendants of enslaved Africans have inherited. There is no amount of money that can break these curses. No amount of politically imposed educational and political opportunities can break these curses. The descendants of enslaved Africans are in dire need of specific information. Their *ignorance* is what is destroying them. Just as in ancient times, living in the Promised Land without the promise is a dangerous proposition, for there will be no constructive parameters within which to live and thrive.

Upon entering the Promise Land phase of their history, Dr. King's people needed to be exposed to the blessing formula and to the two premier principles governing the human experience, *but no one taught them*! This information is critical to the perpetuation of their legacy of freedom and liberation. They can't move into the next phase of their storied history without the blessing formula. They already possess the greatness they need; they just don't know how to access it.

There is no historical record of the Most High delivering any people from the chains of a wicked values system just so they could immediately *embrace* the wickedness from which they were freed. In their hunger to assimilate the values and identities of others, the descendants of enslaved Africans took on the same wicked destiny structure of those who had enslaved their ancestors. They began to view *themselves* through the eyes of their haters. They were *infected* with the hater virus. There is no salvation, socially or spiritually, to be found in the values and identities of others, which is why the descendants of enslaved Africans became so *self*-destructive following their entry into the Promised Land phase of their history.

The perpetuation of their cultural legacy requires the descendants of enslaved Africans to activate the blessing formula in their individual lives. They are supposed to *be* a blessing to the inhabitants of the earth, but what they bring to the table of humanity can only manifest through activation of the blessing formula. They have discredited and skewed their own legacy as a redeemed people by their foolish efforts to graft themselves into the legacies of others. As a result, they are suffering immeasurably. In their efforts to *find* themselves within the frameworks and values associated with the legacies of others, they *lost* themselves. They embraced personal identities based on stereotypical media images, astrological horoscope readings, perverse social expectations, among other things.

The descendants of enslaved Africans became *products* of the whole panoply of social propaganda: projected situations, circumstances, environments and events. As such, they became fuel for the fires of others. They became a prey to the rapacious appetites of vulturous, predatory entities. The descendants of enslaved Africans became so hell-bent on self-destruction through assimilation that others were able to devise creative methods in order to make a profit from their self-conquering lifestyles. Predatory entities work diligently to make it *convenient* for the descendants of enslaved Africans to perpetuate their self-destructive proclivities from one generation to the next. The descendants of enslaved Africans sacrificed the *ultimate* versions of themselves for socially and politically *acceptable* versions. But these versions are limiting, subversive, sometimes illegal, but always *destructive* in some way. Even the successful among them aren't experiencing ultimacy. They're much as Abram and Sarai were: very rich, but unfulfilled.

Meanwhile their "leadership" has enmeshed itself fully within *Canaanite* perspectives. Nobody articulates the *Amalekite* or the *Amorite* state of affairs better than the "leadership" of the descendants of enslaved Africans. Instead of presenting to humanity grander, nobler perspectives, the "leadership" of descendants of enslaved Africans is satisfied to lend their glory to the Jebusites, Girgasites, Hivites and Romans. What a disgrace! When in the Promised Land phase of your history, your relationship with the rest of the world must change.

The reason I have singled out the descendants of enslaved Africans as an example here is that they provide a clear, poignant picture of what the lack of *specific* knowledge can cause, even for those historically in pursuit of freedom and liberation. The descendants of enslaved Africans are a people who've actually *inherited* a legacy of pursuing freedom and liberation on a generational basis. After centuries of bondage, the Most High delivered their ancestors from chattel slavery so that ensuing generations could perpetuate their glorious legacy. Until the Civil Rights Movement, the goals were rather clear-cut. But without the blessing formula, they were unable to proceed effectively beyond that point.

Actually, the descendants of enslaved Africans should be *championing* the blessing formula, exemplifying human liberation at the highest level. Their historical testimony is supposed to be a beacon of *hope* and *truth* for the other inhabitants of the earth. But they have struggled to find their place. Only through activating the blessing formula on an individual basis can they be elevated to their rightful place in the annals of human history, and *be* a blessing to all the inhabitants of the earth.

The enduring lesson for the rest of humanity is that if self-destruction in the absence of the blessing formula can come so heavily among those for whom human liberation is a *legacy*, think of what can and will happen to any other human family, including yours—even in the midst of abundant opportunity.

THE GREAT WALL

The journey of your personal destiny is a long and winding one. Since the enemy cannot curse you, he's depending on you to curse yourself by embracing an identity other than the one revealed by your personal blessing. A lesser personal identity is a curse; it's *sin*. It is equivalent to witchcraft and it provokes the Almighty to anger. Why is this? The Most High has placed an extraordinary vision within you. As such, there is *greatness* within you. When you embrace any personal identity contrary to or less than your personal blessing, you're rejecting the marvelous individual you were created to be. You're not in this life alone. Others are counting on your victory. They are depending on you to operate fully in your personal blessing, and to hand this sacred formula to ensuing generations.

There are daunting realities in life that are overwhelming in appearance. These realities, however, don't determine your victory or defeat. Situation-assessment and self-assessment must always be kept separate. You must erect a wall in your mind between these two assessments. They must never be allowed to mix. What you detect with your natural senses must never determine or alter your personal identity. Never allow what you detect with your natural senses to contaminate your self-concept. First, what you *sense* at any given time is subject to change from one moment to the next. Second, others can *control* situations, circumstances, environments and events. Others can control projected realities and social propaganda. If you don't erect a separating wall in your mind between what you *detect* with your natural senses and what you *are* inwardly, you'll be compromised. You'll be made a slave to the appearances of things, like Pavlov's dog, ever responding to the real or imagined arbitrary stimuli provided by others. You'll absorb and then reflect the projections of others and not even realize that you're doing it. Failure to keep situation-assessment and self-assessment separate is like selling your soul.

When Moses sent the spies into the Promised Land to bring back a reconnaissance assessment, what exactly did they do wrong? What was it about their "evil report" that provoked God to anger? Were they lying about the presence of giants in the land? No, the giant descendants of Anak were indeed there. Moses commanded his spies to assess the situation, and they followed his orders. This isn't what they did wrong. What they did wrong was pollute their *self*-assessment with the information gathered in their *situation*-assessment. In reference to the giants, they reported, "We were in our own sight as grasshoppers, and so we were in their sight."[54] You must always be prepared to be what you are against the backdrop of something that completely *contradicts* your internal reality. The spies allowed their situation-assessment to contaminate and then *dominate* their self-assessment. Their contaminated self-concept was contrary to the highest version of them: *a peculiar treasure unto God above all peoples.* They allowed their collective identity of victory to be contaminated by their situation-assessment, which in turn contaminated their collective destiny structure. They allowed extreme contradictions to intimidate them and, as a result, it affected their state of mind; it affected their perspective; it affected their agenda; it affected their attitude; it

---

[54]   NUMBERS 13:33

affected their aura; it affected their words and it affected their actions. For this, they were condemned to the wilderness for *40 years*.

After Moses pointed out their transgression, out of shame they attempted to take military action, but were handily defeated. Why were they so easily thwarted? They were defeated in battle because they were defeated *already* in their collective identity. They saw themselves as grasshoppers to other men. Don't attempt monumental action if you're not willing to be monumental—*beforehand*, even when there isn't any outward evidence of your monumental status. Don't try to *do* greatly without first *being* great. Greatness only emerges *from* the great, just as victory only emerges *from* the victorious and championships only emerge *from* champions. These are the great truths of the blessing phenomenon.

Attempted monumental action taken out of pure will or intention—absent *being* monumental—lacks authenticity and has no power. The Israelites were ready, willing and able *to* fight, but their contaminated self-concept sapped them of their ability to fight *effectively*. Empty action has no force, and can produce no genuine sustainability or continuity. Hollow action isn't endowed with the spirit of authentic glory. Any strategy that emerges from this vacuity will be wanting. Empty action, based on the exigencies of momentary situations, circumstances, environments or events, has no substantive power. It's not proactive, but *reactive*—going through the motions dictated at any moment by arbitrary stimuli. Hollow action has to it no edge, no advantage, and is wholly ineffective.

You must build an impenetrable wall between your identity of victory and any other assessment you make. Everything is *relative* and *titular* to your personal blessing. You must vehemently guard against the dilution and pollution of your victorious identity. You must never allow your personal identity to be mutated, twisted or compromised in any way by what you're experiencing in your natural senses. In the valiant words of Caleb, one of Moses' faithful spies, you are "well able"[55] to overcome any obstacle, because you are what your personal blessing says you are, right here, right now, *in this very moment!* There can be no compromise on this point—ever. Don't curse yourself! Remain true; be obedient to the *ultimate* version of you. "[T]o obey is better than sacrifice . . ."[56] Victory, fulfillment and peace of mind in every aspect of life will be the result of absolute obedience to the *ultimate version* of you. The highest possible living experience available to you will *pursue* you and *overtake* you if you keep your self-assessment and your situation-assessment separate.

GO YOUR OWN WAY

"[T]he most High ruleth in the kingdom of men, and giveth it to whomsoever he will, and setteth up over it the basest of men."[57] Your personal blessing reveals a path that is particular to *you*. It's not a path of the masses or of the group. It isn't

---

55   NUMBERS 13:30
56   I SAMUEL 15:22
57   DANIEL 4:17

a path consistent with expectations, stigmas or stereotypes. It's unique and special, paved specifically for *you* by the Most High. Your path is an individualized one; it's yours alone. There is no precedent for the path you've been given to travel. Only *you* can walk it; only *you* can experience it. The glow of your personal blessing is what will light your way. Your faithfulness is necessary. The blessing instincts revealed by your destiny structure will guide you. You must be strong enough to separate yourself and go your *own* way. Your separation may be psychological, spiritual, philosophical, physical or emotional. Whatever the case, you must go your *own* way and experience a new life. You must experience a glorious state of mind; a glorious perspective; a glorious agenda; a glorious attitude; a glorious aura; glorious words; glorious actions and, ultimately, glorious fruit. You must go your *own* way. You must experience in full the greatness of your own personal blessing. Your destiny is beckoning, and you must go.

In the great history of the blessing experience, individuals have had to muster the strength and courage to go their own ways. God told Abram to "Get thee out of thy country, and from thy kindred . . ."[58] Rebekeh told Jacob to "[A]rise, flee thou to Laban my brother to Haran."[59] Joseph's brothers said, "Come, and let us sell him to the Ishmeelites . . ."[60] Although he easily could have, notice that even many years later, Joseph never returned to his father's house. He went on to flourish as a prince in the land of Egypt. Before his role as a prophet, "Moses

---

[58] GENESIS 12:1
[59] GENESIS 27:43
[60] GENESIS 37:27

fled from the face of Pharaoh . . ."[61] The Most High commanded Joshua to "[A]rise, go over this Jordan . . ."[62] After the angel revealed his personal blessing to a hiding Gideon, calling him a "mighty man of valour,"[63] the Almighty told Gideon to "Go in this thy might . . ."[64] Gideon was being told to "be *true* to the ultimate version of you." "Michal let David down through a window: and he went, and fled, and escaped."[65] As in these examples, you *too* must be willing to march on triumphantly in fulfillment of your own unique destiny.

"[B]e thou strong and very courageous . . ."[66] Your personal blessing is a life-changing event. It moves you dramatically into another direction, into another phase of life. You have to *"man-up"* when it comes to your personal blessing. This is what the process requires of you. Don't allow yourself to be intimidated and torn between two assessments. Maintain your elevated self-concept, and be true to it. Flee from the curse with all your might by wholeheartedly remaining in the spirit of your personal blessing. Understand that identity produces destiny. Discover your personal blessing by answering the Blessing Question. Embrace those answers as the unique dimensions of your personal identity *right now*, with absolute confidence. Shine with the glory of your personal blessing at all times by operating in it fully for the rest of your life. We don't know what's inside of you, but we do know that we need it. We're all

---

[61] EXODUS 2:15
[62] JOSHUA 1:2
[63] JUDGES 6:12
[64] JUDGES 6:14
[65] I SAMUEL 19:12
[66] JOSHUA 1:7

depending on you to see your personal blessing through to full manifestation.

"No man, having put his hand to the plough, and looking back, is fit for the kingdom of God."[67] Don't look back at your previous personal identity, but look ever forward to your new identity and what it's producing. Consider not the interpretation of your natural senses. Turn your back and walk away from everything inconsistent with your personal blessing. Peter walked successfully upon the sea until he considered himself *in light* of the interpretation of his natural senses. Only then did he begin to sink. Go forward in your victory. By looking back or around, you'll miss what you should be experiencing. Lot's wife looked back and was thereby destroyed. There is something genuinely authenticating about moving forward confidently in your identity of victory, on your own path. This isn't to suggest that you shouldn't remember where you came from. But it's one thing to remember and quite another to wallow nostalgic in a former identity. You can't arrive at where you're going looking back with longing at what you've abandoned. Live completely in your personal blessing, the *ultimate* version of you, and you'll see where you need to be.

David's victorious living experience was very interesting. He had a vicious hater. Saul, his own king, wanted to kill him, and David was aware. David and his best friend, Jonathan, the king's son, wept together when they confirmed Saul's evil designs. David had to go his *own* way; he had to leave the kingdom. His destiny structure, played out against the backdrop of extreme contradictions, revealed an arduous but unique path that he

---

[67]   LUKE 9:62

alone had to follow. He maintained the integrity of his personal blessing in spite of the contrary appearance of things.

David's life eventually came into full bloom. In the course of time, his path led him to a glorious high throne. Throughout the centuries, *multitudes* have been blessed by David's victorious experience—even to this day. Such will be the case for you if you will go your *own* way. Don't forfeit the fruit of your personal blessing; don't abdicate your throne; don't dilute or pollute yourself; don't curse yourself!

The way of the blessing is to "hearken diligently" to the path set before you. This sacred formula requires a renewed lifestyle, but fear not. You are a trustee of this great family treasure. Live it out, and pass the blessing formula to the other inhabitants of the earth and down to your descendants. Participate fully in being a blessing to humanity. Propagate this inheritance as an executor of the blessing estate. Your curse is no more. You are extraordinarily blessed and, as such, you are *free*—at last. Hallelujah.

AFTER WORD

This is the Great Kingdom, the greatest kingdom and civilization of all time! Since 1995, the year of its founding, propagating the revelation articulated in this text has been the *sole* agenda of the Great Kingdom. In the grand historical competition that is human civilization, it is unacceptable for the largest Christian civilization in the world to be amorphous—identifiably invisible. If just *one* Christian is the light of the world and the salt of the earth, then what does an entire *civilization* of Christians constitute? This work serves notice that this great kingdom, this great civilization, as a holy institution, is alive, well and flourishing.

Will this civilization *ever* be surpassed in terms of its glorious identity? its purpose? its nobility? I don't see how it *can* be. Can it be matched? I *expect* that it will be. The standard has now been established. Let the historical record reflect that a righteous *standard* of human civilization on earth, in Christ, stands upon the earth. This civilization marks by far the high point of man's storied history. This kingdom is committed to bringing man face-to-face with the *ultimate* version of himself, one individual at a time. Where on earth is this civilization's competition? Where is this kingdom's competition? Until revealed otherwise, the Great Kingdom *remains* the greatest kingdom and civilization ever established in the history of man. This is no empty declaration. Let us roll out the scroll of human history and compare.

Our kingdom is a *theocracy*, but not of human control. It's not here to control or dominate the lives of its citizens, nor does it *seek* to do so. This kingdom is committed solely to propagating the sacred formula of the blessing of Abraham unto the inhabitants of the earth, in the name of *Yashua*, the actual name of *Jesus*.

This kingdom is here to inspire, uplift and motivate. It is here to encourage, guide and comfort. Our King gave us a new law—the Law of Love—upon which to establish our lives and all our endeavors. In the words of the King himself, "A new commandment I give unto you, That ye love one another; as I have loved you, that ye also love one another. By this shall all men know that ye are my disciples . . ."[68] This is the law upon which anything purported to be a Christian entity must be based. Anything *less* is deception and fraudulence under the shroud of being a *Christian* entity.

It is irrelevant that professed Christians have brought forth this or that institution or thing. Their bringing it forth is not what determines whether it is a *Christian* entity. The Law of Christ is the legal foundation of *anything* Christian. The law upon which an entity is based determines what *manner* of entity it is, not its founders' personal professions of faith and such. Don't be deceived by rapacious, predatory entities that

---

[68] JOHN 13:34-35

spawn madness and confusion in the name of Jesus. The Law of Christ is not some abstract, esoteric, titular law, relegated to the personal lives of Christians or to our sanctuaries at times of worship. In a Christian civilization, the Law of Christ is the *law of the land!* We must not be ashamed of acknowledging, proclaiming and establishing it as such. In fact, it is our *duty* to do so, and to exemplify it fully. No, we cannot *enforce* it—nor do we seek to—but we can *establish* it as the standard upon the earth. For if there is no *standard*, then there's nothing for people to measure up to.

All authority was given to the Christ, the risen savior, both in heaven *and* on earth.[69] So the Law of Christ is higher and more legitimate than *any* other law made by man, past, present or future. Why then shouldn't we be more *serious* about the propagation of our law as others are about theirs? We must not be spiritual cowards. The Great Demographic Kingdom of Christians upon the Earth is the most splendid institutional representation of the Law of Christ the world has ever witnessed. It is the most extraordinary geographical manifestation ever to grace the face of the earth. This kingdom is committed to spreading THE FORMULA; the Holy Book of this Millennium, to all the inhabitants of the earth, for this book contains the sacred formula of the blessing of Abraham.

The inhabitants of this civilization, regardless of color, culture, nationality, language or denomination are Royal Citizens of the Great Kingdom—and nothing less. As such, everyone living in this great kingdom should possess a personal copy of THE FORMULA, which contains the keys to our

[69] MATTHEW 28:18

individual personal inheritances. It is unconscionable for there to be more *Christians* in this kingdom living in defeat than there are persons here who have not heard the Christian message.

Finally, it is in the Spirit of our King, our Law and our activated personal blessings that we the Royal Citizens of the Great Kingdom present this sacred formula, our solemn gift, to *all* the inhabitants of the earth.

"Drop down, ye heavens, from above, and let the skies pour down righteousness: let the earth open, and let them bring forth salvation, and let righteousness spring up together; I the Lord have created it. Woe unto him that striveth with his Maker! Let the potsherd strive with the potsherds of the earth. Shall the clay say to him that fashioneth it, What makest thou? or thy work, He hath no hands?"[70]

---

[70]   ISAIAH 45:8-9

NOTES

NOTES

NOTES

NOTES

CPSIA information can be obtained at www.ICGtesting.com
Printed in the USA
LVOW090805080312

272066LV00002B/12/P